# BEYOND
# ENDURANCE

ALSO BY THE AUTHOR

*Sea of Dreams*

# BEYOND ENDURANCE

### 300 BOATS, 600 MILES, AND ONE DEADLY STORM

## ADAM MAYERS

McCLELLAND & STEWART

**Library and Archives Canada Cataloguing in Publication**

Mayers, Adam
 Beyond endurance : 300 boats, 600 miles, and one deadly storm / Adam Mayers.

ISBN 978-0-7710-5755-7

 1. Fastnet Race.   2. Yachting accidents – Irish Sea.   3. Search and rescue operations – Irish Sea.   4. Survival after airplane accidents, shipwrecks, etc. I. Title.

GV832.M37 2007      797.1'40916337      C2006-904286-1

We acknowledge the financial support of the Government of Canada through the Book Publishing Industry Development Program and that of the Government of Ontario through the Ontario Media Development Corporation's Ontario Book Initiative. We further acknowledge the support of the Canada Council for the Arts and the Ontario Arts Council for our publishing program.

Typeset in Bembo by M&S, Toronto
Printed and bound in Canada

This book is printed on acid-free paper that is 100% recycled, ancient-forest friendly (100% post-consumer recycled).

McClelland & Stewart Ltd.
75 Sherbourne Street
Toronto, Ontario
M5A 2P9
www.mcclelland.com

1 2 3 4 5     11 10 09 08 07

*For Leigh: best friend and most gentle critic*

# Contents

# 1979 Fastnet Who's Who

### Evergreen

Don Green, 45: Skipper and owner. Entrepreneur.

Dennis Aggus, 31: Film and photographic paper salesman.

Ron Barr, 35: High-school teacher.

Dave Downey: Boat manager.

John Fitzpatrick, 45: Head of sales, C&C Yachts.

Alan Jeyes: Accountant.

Steve Killing, 28: Engineer, C&C Yachts.

Al Megarry, 19: Student.

Jim Talmage, 32: Forest products sales.

### Magistri

Chuck Bentley, 37: Skipper, co-owner. Custom sales, C&C Yachts.

Arch Alyea, 34: Engineer, M.B.A.

Andre Calla, 27: Architecture student.

Peter Cowern, 32: Financial analyst, Ford Canada.

Nick DeGrazia, 36: Dean, University of Detroit.

Peter Farlinger, 39: Co-owner. Entrepreneur.

Fred Goode, 37: Co-owner. RCMP officer.

Dennis Hogarth: Co-owner. Accountant.

Lt. John Hollidge, 29: Royal Navy.

Peter Milligan, 30: Co-owner. Real estate lawyer.

Chris Punter, 32: Co-owner. Crown prosecutor.

### Pachena

John Newton, 49: Skipper, owner. Entrepreneur.

Stewart Jones, 25: Graduate student.

Pat Leslie: Air Canada pilot.

Don Martin, 33: Marine architect.

Doug Race, 34: Lawyer.

Glenn Shugg, 25: Financial management.

John Simonett, 37: Marine engineer.

Mike Schnetzler, 32: Mechanical engineer.

Steve Tupper, 38: Coach, Canada's sailing team.

### Magic

Peter Whipp, 30: Skipper and owner. Accountant.

Tim Allison, 30: Farmer.

David Bootham

Peter Hoosen-Owen, 35: Grammar-school teacher.

John Franklin

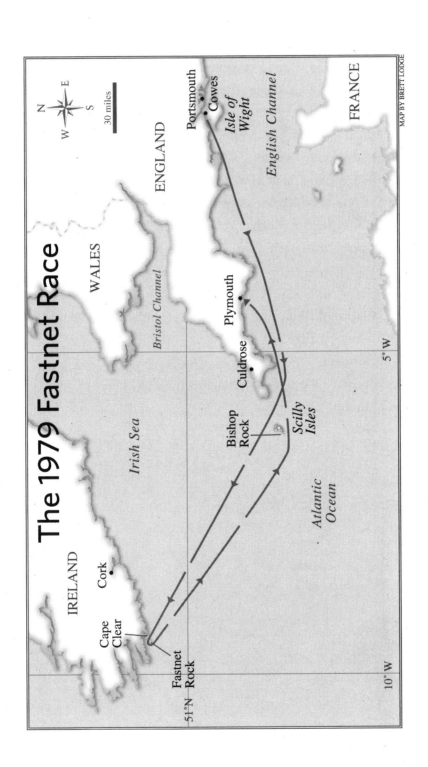

The 1979 Fastnet Race

IRELAND

Cork

Cape
Clear

Fastnet
Rock

51°N

Irish Sea

WALES

Bristol Channel

ENGLAND

Plymouth

Culdrose

Bishop
Rock

Scilly
Isles

Atlantic
Ocean

Portsmouth

Cowes

Isle of
Wight

English Channel

FRANCE

10°W

5°W

N
W        E
S

30 miles

MAP BY BRETT LODGE

# *Preface*

In August 1979, I lived in Cawsand, a village in Cornwall on the southwest coast of England and worked at the *Western Morning News*, a newspaper in nearby Plymouth. Winston Churchill had been a special correspondent for the *Morning News* during the Boer War, and as this was my first full-time job after a year of postgraduate studies in London, I considered myself lucky to be following in such footsteps. A path led from Cawsand along a tree-lined road to Penlee Point, a rocky cliff overlooking Plymouth Sound, the bay that shelters the city from the English Channel. A crumbling watchtower offered a sunny vantage point for viewing the traffic far below. I could picture the great events that had taken place here: Sir Francis Drake waiting for a favourable tide to take his fleet into the Channel to meet the Spanish Armada in 1588; the Pilgrim Fathers boarding the *Mayflower* in 1620, seeking religious and political freedom in the New World. At the height of the Napoleonic Wars, Lord Nelson's fleet sailed to Plymouth to be resupplied and refitted after blockade duty along the French coast. In the fall of 1940 until the spring of 1941, the Luftwaffe fire-bombed Plymouth in an effort to destroy the naval base as a prelude to Operation Sea Lion, the Nazi invasion of Britain.

In the early part of August 1979, another chapter in the story of Plymouth and the sea was being written. The Admiral's Cup, a series of ocean races that culminates in a 605-mile race to the Fastnet Rock lighthouse off the south coast of Ireland and back, was underway and three Canadian boats had been entered as a team.

The *Hamilton Spectator* sent Stewart Brown to cover the team, and when he arrived in Plymouth he invited me to lunch. I had worked at the *Spectator* and looked forward to catching up on the news. We never did have lunch together because near hurricane-force winds descended on the fleet, resulting in nineteen deaths – fifteen among the competitors – the abandonment of twenty-four boats – five of which sank – and the rescue of 136 people. Of the 303 boats that started the race, 218 did not finish, and the 1979 Fastnet remains the worst disaster in the sport of ocean-racing.

At the time, I was struck as much by the many accounts of individual and collective heroism as I was by the fury of nature that awful night. The crews were for the most part quite ordinary people, Sunday sailors, who exceeded their normal abilities and did extraordinary things. How were they able to do that? And what was the personal cost of such an extreme test?

These questions resurfaced while I was writing *Sea of Dreams*, the story of the 2002 Around Alone race, in which Canadian Derek Hatfield circumnavigated the globe in a race that nearly cost him his life. The themes of exceptional abilities, heroism, and tragedy were similar in many ways, and I decided to delve into the Fastnet race to explore them further.

The one best-selling book about the Fastnet tragedy was a first-person account by noted sailing journalist John Rousmaniere, *Fastnet, Force 10*. I set out to find as many Canadian sailors who had survived the race as I could to recreate their experience, as well as the crew of one English boat rescued by a Canadian boat that night. *Beyond Endurance* is based on multiple interviews with those twenty-six men who were part of the Admiral's Cup campaign. They are in middle and advanced age, and most live in Canada and the United States. Their recollections were detailed, vivid, and frank. Some felt they had not risen to the occasion and still feel guilty; some suffered delayed traumatic reactions; none gave up sailing as a result. About half came back to do the race again. Most regard the experience as one of the most exhilarating moments of their life.

In some places, the recollections differed in detail, though rarely in substance. In those instances, I describe what I believe happened. Any mistakes therefore are mine.

Without exception, the men in this story came away from the race feeling more alive, knowing more about themselves, feeling more confident and more grounded. Some described surviving the race as a spiritual experience. Many say the event profoundly changed them and that what was important after the race was different from what had been important before it. The epiphany often came at the worst moment of the night.

In the end, the sailors who are the focus of this book did not beat the storm. But they are heroes, for they did not let it beat them, and when people go out to sea in small boats that is all you can do.

# I

# Saturday Morning

**"Twenty years from now you will be more disappointed by the things that you didn't do than by the ones you did do."**

– MARK TWAIN

$T$HE BOATS WERE stacked ten deep at the end of the docks in front of the Royal Ocean Yacht Squadron. It was early morning on Saturday, August 11, 1979, but the basin in Cowes, on the Isle of Wight, was full of anxious sailors doing the last-minute fidgeting that precedes all races. In addition to the fifty-six Admiral's Cup boats waiting to start the Fastnet race, there were almost 250 other boats of all shapes and sizes, some with very experienced crews and others crewed by men eager to earn a stripe or two. This was the big time and they were here.

The race hadn't encountered any real trouble in twenty years, and this year the fleet was the largest ever assembled, an armada of 303 boats with about three thousand sailors, all looking forward to a challenging ride, exhilarating even, if the wind blew hard. It promised to be a 605-mile midsummer romp along the south coast of England and into the tail of the North Atlantic. Most hoped that the wind would blow, because that would really test their seamanship, their boats, and their competitive spirit. It was, after all, a race.

The race widely reckoned to have been the worst was a distant memory now, a nasty affair in 1957 with gale-force winds so strong that of the forty-one boats that started, three-quarters quit within a hundred miles. The American yacht *Carina II* stuck it out and won, although a few ribs in her wooden hull were cracked early on and her crew had to man her bilge pumps all the way around the course. When she crossed the finish line, her skipper, Dick S. Nye, removed the stump of a cigar from his mouth and said, "Okay, boys, you can let her sink now." Nye won the Fastnet again in 1975, and this time around, at age seventy-six, he was joined by his son and grandson on another *Carina.* That's how much sailors enjoyed this race.

At the other extreme, the race could be maddeningly slow if the wind didn't pipe up, which was as often as not the case. The last three runnings had been drifters, not much fun at all. Everyone agreed that what the race had was an enviable record of safety. There had only ever been one fatality, in 1977 when a middle-aged man died of a heart attack.

Don Green, the skipper of the Canadian boat *Evergreen,* was among the few who were not expecting much from the coming competition. The series of Admiral's Cup races leading up to this finale had been a disappointment. For eighteen months, his forty-one-foot custom-built sloop had been the other woman in his life, but he no longer loved her quite as much as he once did. He had adorned his mistress with all the high-tech trinkets money could buy, and a year earlier he had been rewarded with a victory on Lake St. Clair in an international competition. It had been a day to remember. This series, however, had been one disappointment after the other.

As Green went about the last-minute business of readying the boat, his outward calm and encouraging comments to the crew belied his concerns about *Evergreen's* condition. Had anyone looked into his brown eyes they would have seen his worry and indecision. Though tough and determined and not afraid to make difficult decisions alone, Green preferred to manage by consensus because it often yielded the best results. In this case, he needed to know how committed the crew was, how much they still wanted to compete, and how resilient their spirits were before he took them off into a final adventure in the North Atlantic. When they gave him the nod, he agreed to go.

*Evergreen* had been designed to perform best in light wind, the predominant summer pattern on her Lake Ontario home. In the English Channel, she had faced two weeks of high winds, the sort of conditions where at home the boat would stay tied up at the dock. In the Solent, the channel that separates the Isle of Wight from the mainland, sailing downwind in the tidal race, with all her sails flying, the boat had been like a Frisbee, the hull swaying back and forth as the helmsman tried to keep her from tipping over. *Evergreen* had run aground twice, smashing her keel on one of the many rocky shoals in these waters. The repair had been hasty and crude, and Green didn't know what that had done for her stability and speed. Her mast was also a worry. It was a thin, experimental rig that had so far stayed up, but it had broken the previous summer in much lighter winds than those seen so far. *Evergreen* was ill-equipped to handle winds of fifteen knots and down-right danger-ous in twenty-five knots. Now she was about to head out into the open ocean for three, maybe four days.

*Evergreen* was one of three boats, along with *Magistri* and *Pachena*, that formed the Canadian team, and after two weeks of competition, the team wasn't doing well at all, sitting seventeenth out of the nineteen countries. Only Poland and Brazil's teams were faring worse. Despite the standing, the Canadians were proud just to be there because the Admiral's Cup races, of which the Fastnet was the last, were by invitation only. They were the Olympics of the ocean-racing world, a two-week-long competition culminating in the race to the Fastnet Rock, a jumble of stone with a lighthouse on top, just ten miles off the Irish Coast. There, the fleet would turn around and come back.

(*Manitou I*, a fourth Canadian boat that had sailed to England just to do the Fastnet, would retire soon after the race started when a shroud supporting the mast broke. An inspection revealed a hairline crack in the mast, so she returned to port. *Manitou IV* hailed from Toronto's National Yacht Club and was owned by Oakville's Ken Merron. She later sailed back across the Atlantic.)

The Cup was held every two years in the first two weeks of August, coinciding with Cowes Race Week, the annual highlight of the British sailing calendar and the longest-running regular regatta in the world. Each day, there were at least thirty-five different races with as many as nine hundred boats taking part, not including the Admiral's Cup races, which were squeezed in as part of the festivities.

The three-boat Admiral's Cup national teams had been invited to compete based on their performance in trials either in their home country or in other ocean races. This was the second time the Canadians had been invited. In 1975, *Diva* and *Dinamo* (both Ontario boats) and *Kanata* (from Vancouver) had placed eighteenth out of nineteen teams. A few of those sailors were back again.

The Admiral's Cup comprised a week of practice, a tune-up race, two thirty-mile inshore events in the Solent, and then a 220-mile cross-Channel race to France and back. The Fastnet finale was expected to take anywhere between three days and a week, depending on conditions.

The Fastnet race was first run in 1925 and arose from the notion that yachting had to be open to more than just a few very rich men with paid crews racing against other very rich men. So the race was designed for the amateur who wanted a challenge beyond cruising. Typically, he was the skipper with a crew of a few friends or hired help. Seven boats entered that first race, which was won by *Jolie Brise*, a fifty-six-foot cutter that completed the course in a little under seven days. The inaugural event was deemed so successful that it led to the formation of the Ocean Racing Club, which later received a "Royal" designation, made its headquarters at Cowes, and had organized the race ever since.

In 1957, five British sailors challenged a group of American friends to additional races in the Solent, and the Admiral's Cup was born. The Royal Ocean Racing Club (RORC) took over responsibility and, in 1959, opened the event to teams from any country. It quickly became known as one of the toughest of the various challenges that form the international ocean-racing circuit. By the start of the 1979 series, Britain had won the Cup seven out of eleven times; the United States twice; and Germany and Australia once each.

The British were favoured this time, and the team most likely to stop them was the American one, which included Dennis Conner, a bronze-medal winner in the Tempest class at the Montreal Olympics. Conner had already won his first America's Cup and was on the rise as a world player. He was a professional sailor, a harbinger of things to come. Conner was driving *Williwaw*, a forty-five-footer that had been the overall winner of the Admiral's

Cup in 1977. Ted Turner, the founder of Cable Network News (CNN), was planning to race just the Fastnet in sixty-foot *Tenacious*, with a crew that included his sixteen-year-old son Teddy Jr.

The Canadians didn't expect to win but hoped to improve their skills, learn the ropes of the international game, and have some fun. The previous decade had seen a resurgence of interest in sailing in Canada, inspired by the around-the-world exploits of single-handers such as Sir Francis Chichester and Sir Robin Knox-Johnston. C&C Yachts in Oakville, Ontario, had become one of North America's leading boat builders, among the first to mass-produce fibreglass cruising yachts. C&C was about to open a plant in Rhode Island to serve the American market. The company's cachet with cruising sailors depended in large part on turning out winning race designs, so C&C was usually involved in plans by the ocean-sailing elite to build newer and faster boats.

That was why Don Green had gone to C&C, taking an enormous gamble by commissioning *Evergreen*. She was a one-off experiment, technically a full fifteen years ahead of her time, and costing the equivalent of about $1 million (Canadian) today. When she didn't quite live up to Green's expectations, he spent even more money to fix the problems, long after others told him to write the boat off and start again. The changes turned her into a hot rod that blew the doors off the competition on the Great Lakes and brought honour and glory to Canada, defeating an American team in the 1978 Canada's Cup, the oldest sporting event between the two countries.

Winning that event appealed to many aspects of Green's personality. An unabashed nationalist, he loved challenges and overcoming obstacles. It had been an expensive victory, but fortunately Green could afford it, since he owned a car-parts company in

Hamilton, Ontario, that he had grown from a father-and-son operation into a multinational called Tridon Ltd., with plants in Canada, the United States, and Europe.

The good news for Green that Saturday morning was that the long-range forecast was for benign conditions in the early going with the potential for a bit of a rough ride on the homeward leg. Even so, he did not relish the idea of venturing into the open ocean in *Evergreen*, and if he had had his druthers he would have packed up then and there and gone home. But he did not want to hurt Canada's reputation and perhaps its chances of being invited back in 1981. He had sailed through a typhoon as a young man during a year-long circumnavigation, so he knew how vicious and unmerciful the sea could be. He weighed the pros and cons and after talking them over with the crew was still undecided. "I really did not want to do the Fastnet," he says, "but in the end, I agreed to go."

His mood had been much brighter two weeks earlier when the crew arrived in Cowes. *Evergreen* represented everything that was the future. She was made of fibreglass rather than wood, synthetic fabric rather than canvas, and had a stripped-down interior, a wide flat bottom, and electronics that included an on-board computer. Her most radical feature was an adjustable keel that slid up and down like a daggerboard in a dinghy. Green had not expected huge differences between races held on Lake St. Clair and the south coast of England.

*Evergreen*'s nine-man crew was feeling invincible. They were really just big kids. The youngest was nineteen, and many of the others had just started their first real jobs, yet as a group they had an unshakeable faith in their abilities. The other Canadians noticed their light steps and easy jokes, and knew the proof would come soon enough. The nine-man crew had been together for less than eighteen months, and only two or three of them had sailed with

*Evergreen's* Admiral's Cup team. From left: Hans Fogh, Alan Jeyes, Jim
Talmage, Dave Downey, Al Megarry, John Fitzpatrick, Steve Killing,
Don Green, Rob Ball, Dennis Aggus. Ron Barr is missing from the
photo, and neither Fogh nor Ball sailed in the Fastnet race. (*Team photo*)

Green before that. They were good at day racing, but less experienced in ocean conditions than the crews of the other Canadian
boats. They didn't know how they would behave under real stress
because they had never faced any crisis as a team. They knew less
about how their boat would behave at the extremes of weather for
the same reason.

The senior team members were more humble in their expectations, knowing that the race was more than a step-up the competitive ladder. John Bobyk had been to Great Lakes regattas and was
part of *Evergreen's* support team. When he stepped off the ferry at
Cowes, he saw just how different this race was. The yacht basin was
filled with boats as far as the eye could see, the sort of boats one saw
in sailing magazines and wondered who could afford to buy them.

Well, the buyers were here, row upon row of them: the wealthy, the powerful, the privileged. Smartly dressed men and women clinking glasses, filling the air with hearty laughter. It made him feel like a country boy whose feet had struck pavement for the first time.

# 2

# *Rivalries*

**"To be on the wire is life. The rest is waiting."**

– TIGHTROPE WALKER KARL WALLENDA

~~~~~~~~~~~~~~~~
~~~~~~~~~~~~~~~~

*T*HE FINAL FASTNET race briefing for skippers took place midmorning on August 11, several hours before the 1:15 p.m. start. It was the usual combination of warnings and reminders, a long-range weather forecast qualified by a lot of maybes, which left the skippers with the impression that the first few days would be quite pleasant – light wind and sunny skies – followed by the possibility of a bad stretch by Tuesday. How bad, it was hard to tell. Satellite photos showed a system moving across the Atlantic from Newfoundland, but it was weakening. Another system was moving southeast from Iceland. If they intersected, the fleet could expect high winds and rain – a short, nasty blow – but it looked as if the centre of the combined system would veer to the north and pass over southern Ireland. Nobody entering the race expected to have trouble with the conditions.

*Magistri's* skipper, Chuck Bentley, came away from the briefing believing it would be just more of the same. After what they had seen in two weeks of competition, they doubted that the weather could get much worse. They figured that if the British and French routinely raced in the conditions they had just been through, then it must be possible, and if it were possible they could do it. "We looked at one another and said, 'Let's go,'" says Bentley, a former high-school teacher turned professional sailor.

*Magistri* sailed out of Toronto's Royal Canadian Yacht Club (RCYC) and, like *Evergreen*, was designed by C&C. But that was where the similarities ended. *Evergreen* had been in the water for eighteen months, *Magistri* for five years. *Evergreen* was light as a feather, *Magistri* was a traditional, heavy, full-ballasted boat. *Evergreen* was bankrolled by one wealthy man, *Magistri* by the six friends who owned the boat, including Bentley. Although *Magistri* flew the RCYC burgee, several crew hailed from Toronto's more casual National Yacht Club. Some weren't members of any sailing club, and more than a few had never owned a boat. Some of *Magistri's* crew of eleven had sailed together for a decade or more, through good times and bad, broken marriages, untold cases of beer, and in every kind of weather imaginable. She had squeaked in as the third boat on the team after a great winter in Florida. There in the so-called Southern Ocean Racing Circuit (SORC), the place where racing sailors go in January and February to keep their oars in, they had put on a show. But five-year-old cars rarely win Grand Prix races.

*Magistri's* crew came from different backgrounds, but was united by bonds of friendship, a love of competitive sailing, and the Darwinian process of selection that had brought them together. Prospects had been invited to sail her, and if they weren't good enough, or their personalities didn't fit, they weren't asked back. A lot of people sailed *Magistri* once or twice and that was it. The core

The *Magistri* team at Cowes. From left, top row: Fred Goode, Paul Dickson, Lt. John Hollidge, Peter Cowern, Peter Farlinger, Chris Punter, Peter Milligan. Bottom row: Nick DeGrazia, Ian Craik, Chuck Bentley, Andre Calla, Dennis Hogarth, Arch Alyea. Dickson and Craik did not sail in the Fastnet. (*Team photo*)

crew wanted a team like themselves, older and fairly quiet, not given to a lot of hollering or hot-dogging, just people who would sail hard and have fun.

Most of them lived and worked in Toronto, although one lived in Detroit and another in Hamilton. None of them was particularly well-heeled or well-connected, although some were members of Canada's most storied and privileged yacht club, a place with deep pools of money and plenty of central Canadian power and influence. Nine of them were either separated or divorced, something that may have been a coincidence but came to be part of the glue that bound them together.

"Sailing wasn't our mistress," says Chris Punter, one of *Magistri*'s six owners. "It was more about the time of our lives. Some of us may have been married too young and made the wrong choices. We just happened to come together and ended up having some unique and remarkable times."

The bachelor's life provided a freedom their friends envied. Every spare evening and weekend could be devoted to grooming *Magistri*. If they wanted to stay late for one more beer, or one beer too many, so what? They were free – give or take a little alimony and child support – at a time when most of their peers were juggling young families and jobs that left little time for recreation.

Soon after *Magistri* was purchased in 1976, the team stripped her down and rebuilt the hull and deck, rewired her circuits, and installed new instruments. She had a dozen doting fathers who indulged her every whim and agonized over her every wheeze and cough. They knew her inside and out, and should anything go wrong, which in sailing usually happens at the worst moment, they could quickly diagnose and repair the problem. They worked hard to get the boat into shape and that effort helped to build the team.

"The act of doing something together builds camaraderie," says Peter Cowern, one of the few team members who was married. The New Zealand native had only recently taken up sailing and embraced it because it met a need for excitement and friendship.

The First Wives Club spent their summers trundling up and down the Great Lakes, starting with major events on Lake Ontario and Lake Erie, then the 235-mile Port-Huron-to-Mackinac race and the "Big Mac," the Chicago-to-Mackinac race, which runs the length of Lake Michigan. An army of willing hands shuttled the boat from race start to race start. On one occasion, they were in such a hurry they sailed from Lake Huron to Chicago using a Michigan road map, guessing at their location by the size of the lights on shore. It worked pretty well. "It was a full summer," says Fred Goode, one of the six owners, then an RCMP officer. "Very demanding."

The toughest race was the Trans Superior. The 338-mile course, for serious sailors only, starts at the east end of the largest and coldest of the Great Lakes and ends in Duluth, Minnesota, two or three days later. *Magistri* won twice, once in 1975 just a few months before the ore carrier *Edmund Fitzgerald* sank in November. They almost suffered the same fate, not far from the same spot, just outside Whitefish Bay, Michigan. *Magistri* was knocked flat in a storm that seemed to come from nowhere and without warning pinned her on her side. For long seconds, as water poured in through open hatches, the crew wondered if the boat was going down. "Lake Superior is the one place where I don't want to go back and sail," says Punter. "It is truly primeval."

In the winters, the crew kicked it up a notch, flying to Florida for long weekends to the SORC races. Today, SORC is a week-long series of races held every February in Miami. In the late 1970s, it included a race between Miami and Nassau and another between St. Petersburg and Ft. Lauderdale, plus a variety of day and overnight races. To gain the experience they needed for ocean racing, the team started practising early in the spring until late in the fall. When the boat came back from Florida each March, it stayed in the water in Port Credit, the closest harbour to Toronto with facilities that were open that time of year. Bundled up like Arctic explorers, the crew dodged chunks of ice to bump their skills up. On days with high waves and a nasty northeaster, when nobody else was out on the lake, they would be out there learning how to sail in heavy weather.

"Everything we had done up to that point, whether we considered it or not, was training for the Admiral's Cup," says crew member Arch Alyea. "In those years, it was the pinnacle, it was something you had to do."

In a sport with equal amounts of big money and big egos, *Magistri* was an anomaly. Goode had recently been seconded from the RCMP to the new Canadian Security Intelligence Service, the civilian spy agency. A tall, strapping, gregarious man, the thirty-seven-year-old Goode hardly seemed like a spy. Outgoing, always up for a party, and between wives, the Nova Scotia native liked to tease his freshwater teammates when the going got rough on Lake Ontario and waves were breaking over the boat by shouting, "Time to pass the salt!"

Dennis Hogarth was an accountant, and Chuck Bentley worked for C&C Yachts, running its custom boat-building division. These three founding owners were joined by Chris Punter, a Crown prosecutor, Peter Farlinger, who owned a small construction company, and Peter Milligan, a lawyer in real estate. All six men threw $10,000 into the pot to buy *Magistri*. She had been built in 1974 and christened *Marauder* by a group chaired by Gordon Fisher, then a senior executive at the Southam newspaper chain. After a disappointing show at the 1975 Canada's Cup, Fisher's group sold her. In the fall of 1976, she was lying in Racine, Wisconsin, which is where Chuck Bentley found her.

That year Bentley's first marriage ended, and after more then a decade teaching high school and sailing on the side, he joined C&C Yachts to make sailing the focus of his life. A tall, wiry man who is at turns gruff and playful, Bentley's great strength as a skipper is his tenacity. He never quits, either because he is too stubborn or because he is so focused he doesn't see the possibility of failure. Friends say he is outspoken and plain-speaking, fair, a good teacher, able to wring the best out of his crew, and a superb yachtsman. The crew liked him and came back year after year to sail with him.

"Some people have an energy about them, and he's the kind of guy you'd follow anywhere," says Peter Milligan. "How he brought all those guys together, a once-in-a-lifetime crew, was a pretty special thing."

One consequence of Bentley's divorce was the sale of a thirty-nine-foot boat, also called *Magistri*. He had raced this boat with the nucleus of those who would form the 1979 team. After it was sold, Bentley's friends proposed a syndicate to buy a new one. So when he came across *Marauder* in Racine, he dragged Goode and Dennis Hogarth down for a look.

*Magistri* was a traditional C&C racing design, forty-two feet long, twelve and a half feet at her widest point, and a hefty twenty thousand pounds. Her seven-and-a-half-foot keel weighed nearly eleven thousand pounds. She needed the weight to counteract the force exerted on her sails. Up front, she carried a large genoa and a balloonlike spinnaker for downwind runs. She had a very tall mast, but by today's standards a very small mainsail, the boat's primary "engine." *Magistri* was narrow at the front and had a pinched high transom at the back. The deck was flat and clear because the winches, including a coffee grinder, were in the cockpit.

After he had spotted her, Bentley called Goode and said he'd found the perfect racing machine. Goode and Hogarth jumped on an airplane and flew to Racine. The $90,000 (U.S.) price tag was a good deal, so they bought it, although it was all they could do to scrape up a down payment.

"I said, 'Where the hell are we going to come up with the rest?'" Goode says. "Dennis said, 'Don't worry.' He was an accountant and was very smart. He said, 'What we need is some bridge financing.' I didn't even know what that was."

The bridge financing turned out to be a friend who had just won a million dollars in a lottery. "We called him up and said, 'How would you like to sail with us?'" Goode says. "He lent us the money, he got to sail, and we were able to close the deal."

Although Bentley owned only one-sixth of the boat, he was the boss. *Magistri* was his boat. It carried the name he chose, Latin for teacher. Although he has spent a life on the water, he has never learned to swim, a fact that comforted his crew. They figured Chuck would do everything to make sure his boat stayed afloat.

Although *Evergreen* and *Magistri* were on the same team, there was a rivalry between them, and during the Admiral's Cup the two crews went their separate ways. The bad feeling baffled the sailors from the third boat, *Pachena*, which hailed from Vancouver. *Evergreen*'s crew shared a house in Cowes on the Isle of Wight with the *Pachena* squad, but the *Magistri* crew had their own house and kept to themselves. By mutual consent, the two groups steered clear of each other.

The animosity stemmed from the Canada's Cup trials the previous year. There had been a no-holds-barred series of races in which Don Green had beaten the RCYC's Paul Phelan and his boat, *Mia V*, for the right to challenge the American champion. Another RCYC boat, Rudy Koehler's *Impetus*, was also involved in the trials, but the series was essentially a two-boat race between Green and Phelan. Although none of the *Magistri* crew had been directly involved in the Cup, a year later they were still feeling the effect of the fallout. The series offered no financial reward to the winner, and the cost of the boats and the campaigns together exceeded what most people earned in a lifetime. When this was put to Green by *Toronto Star* sports reporter Rex MacLeod, Green cryptically replied, "It's expensive, but we don't talk about it."

Those outside the world of yacht racing might consider what happened next petty, trivial, and confirming every stereotype about the behaviour of rich men and their silly games. Green, who sailed out of the Royal Hamilton Yacht Club, upset the order of things. He decided he wanted to challenge the Bayview Yacht Club in Detroit for the Cup. The rules of the game were that if an American club had the Cup, it could be challenged only by a club from Canada.

But the RCYC had always interpreted "a club from Canada" to mean them in perpetuity. Since 1896, they had been the lone Canadian challenger and considered it their inherited right. It was not something that one discussed, it just *was*. So, the club viewed Green's challenge with alarm. Not only was he from out of town, but he was not well known on the racing circuit. Did he understand what was involved? Was he serious? Would he embarrass the country? The RCYC was so upset it refused to provide Green with a copy of the rules and regulations that govern Canada's Cup races. It took Green almost a year to get ahold of the rules, but he did get them. Nothing was going to stop him.

The RCYC had misjudged a man who, despite an unassuming attitude, is tenacious, competitive, and rather enjoys a good fight. You have to have these qualities to turn a family-owned business that makes hose clamps into a multinational car-parts company, which Green had done with Tridon Ltd. The company had consumed all of Green's energy for almost twenty years, but by the early 1970s he had time to spare and returned to sailing. He bought a C&C 38, named it *Motivation*, and started club racing on Wednesdays. He took part in many summer weekend races and gathered a crew of young, enthusiastic sailors around him. When the RCYC started pushing him around, he pushed back.

"The battle with the Royal Canadians was beyond belief," Green says. "It was wild, it was pathetic. Today we laugh and are all very good friends, but back then it was very serious."

The closer it got to the trials that would determine which boat would face the Americans, the nastier it became. The RCYC challenged *Evergreen*'s skipper, Tim Stearn, saying he was ineligible to race because he was an American citizen. The rules said some crew could be non-Canadian, but that others had to be. The RCYC interpreted that as meaning the helmsman must be Canadian, thus disqualifying Stearn. Green threatened to sue, but in the end relented and learned the fine art of helmsmanship. He would steer the boat himself. The gamesmanship was extraordinary, the issues unimportant, but the stakes high.

The warm-up races in June and July 1978 were followed by the main trials in early August. *Evergreen* made short work of the RCYC boats, and Green rubbed it in. He told the *Toronto Star*'s Rex MacLeod with calculated insult that he would have felt better if *Evergreen* had been tested more thoroughly.

"We won so easily that we wonder if we were that fast or they were that slow," he said triumphantly.

*Evergreen* added insult to injury at the Canada's Cup by beating the American boat *Agape* in a thrilling campaign during which *Evergreen* broke her mast and ran aground in Lake St. Clair. For a fleeting moment in the fall of 1978, Don Green and his crew were national heroes.

# 3

# The Show

**"If everything seems under control, you're just not going fast enough."**

– MARIO ANDRETTI

~~~~~~~~~~~~~~~~~~~~

*I*N COWES, as the countdown continued, it was *Magistri*'s crew who felt most confident of the three Canadian boats. They had been within spitting distance of *Evergreen* in every Admiral's Cup race, even beating her in one, reinforcing the feeling of satisfaction and self-confidence after a strong winter in Florida. There, the crew had rubbed shoulders with the main players – Dennis Conner and Ted Turner – and had learned that they were in the same league. The Admiral's Cup had reinforced that view. They were losing, but not by that much, and the Fastnet finale offered the chance for the aging *Magistri* to demonstrate that she deserved to be here.

"It was exciting," says Peter Milligan. "We realized that a bunch of guys who had tossed some money together could go out and sail with the big money. There are a few races you want to do in your life, and the Admiral's Cup was one of them. You'd gone to 'The Show,' as they say in baseball."

*Magic* was moored at the far end of the Cowes basin, one of the smaller boats in the fleet, a pretty thirty-footer with a fin keel and a transom-hung rudder, a custom design built in the Channel Island of Guernsey. She was not a member of an Admiral's Cup team, but was one of the 250 or so other boats that had been entered for the Fastnet race. Her wooden hull and topsides were a burnished blond, shiny from the many loving coats of varnish applied by her owner. She was crewed by a group of friends with coastal sailing experience who enjoyed small-boat racing. They were looking forward to improving their skills during a midsummer regatta in which they had long aspired to compete. They had done all the other shorter races. As one of *Magic*'s crew put it, "It was just our time."

On the Monday, six days earlier, *Magic* had left the Isle of Man in the Irish Sea for the four-hundred-mile journey to the starting line, something that could take three or four days, depending on conditions. Right from the start, it was a nasty ride with rain, grey skies, and unseasonably cold temperatures. Some hours after departure, Peter Whipp, the accountant who owned the boat, noticed that the brackets on which *Magic*'s rudder hung were loose. There was too much play, making steering sloppy. Whipp was concerned enough that he changed course and headed for Dunleary, Ireland, about ninety miles from Man, where they put rubber washers between the hull and the plate, securing the rudder, and tightened everything up. As far as Whipp was concerned, the problem had been solved.

On Tuesday night, *Magic* left Dunleary and had a pleasant overnight sail. By late Wednesday, she was well into the Channel, off Plymouth Sound. Then the wind gradually picked up and kept rising. Before long, it was blowing at gale force against the ebbing tide, building the sea into steep, short, boat-breaking chunks of water.

*Magic* was in trouble, in a storm, in shipping lanes, and unable to make headway. She hove to, a technique that stops the boat and lets it drift slowly. There was still a danger of being run down, and Peter Whipp remembers being unnerved when a cross-Channel ferry thundered by. He raised the boat on the radio and asked for help in making other shipping aware of *Magic*'s presence. "The ferry couldn't believe we were out there in that," Whipp says. "Neither could we."

Soon afterwards, *Magic*'s crew decided to seek shelter and made for Dartmouth, about forty miles northeast. They arrived early Thursday and collapsed. Whipp was worried they wouldn't make the start of the Fastnet race, but as the day wore on, the rain stopped and the wind eased. *Magic* put to sea in late evening.

All three men were exhausted, "absolutely shot," Whipp says, because they hadn't had a full night's sleep in three days. *Magic* had an autopilot, and Whipp plotted a course he hoped would take the boat through the Hurst Narrows, a narrow, half-mile-wide channel between the mainland and the chalk cliffs of the Isle of Wight at the west end of the Solent. His course allowed for current and tides, but since one of the three crew would always be at the helm, his quick calculations could be adjusted as needed.

Peter Hoosen-Owen, a schoolteacher when he wasn't sailing, took the first watch. The boat was happily broad reaching, making eight or nine knots, and those below fell deeply asleep, lulled by the soothing sounds of wind and water. The next thing Whipp remembers was that the sun was up.

"I thought, Bloody hell, Peter's been on watch all night. That's good of him," Whipp recalls. "But when I stuck my head up, Peter was asleep on the floor of the cockpit and we were in the Hurst Narrows. How we managed that and didn't come to grief I do not know."

It was midmorning Friday, one day before the start of the Fastnet race, when they tied up at the dock at the Royal Ocean Yacht Squadron. Whipp and his friends had barely twenty-four hours to get cleaned up and put *Magic* in order. They picked up David Bootham and John Franklin, who had made their own ways to Cowes.

At the final briefing, the skippers were given details of the course, including the location of the marks to be rounded and such hazards as rocks and shoals. There were reminders about safety, and the Admiral's Cup skippers were told what the radio protocol was and how often they should report their positions. Admiral's Cup boats were required to have a VHF radio that could both send and receive. The non-Cup boats were only required to have a radio that could receive weather forecasts. They were not required to check in, and once they set sail were not expected to be heard from until they finished.

The briefing ran through the shopping list of safety gear required on board: flares and life jackets, man-overboard life rings, and harnesses that can be attached to fixed points on the deck or a jackline. Jacklines were not a requirement, but many boats had them as a matter of course. These are lengths of webbing that run the length of the boat on either side. In rough weather, harnesses can be clipped to the line, allowing sailors to move on deck to change or adjust sails but still be tied to the boat. All the boats also had to have a life raft, running lights, fire extinguishers, a first-aid kit, and emergency rations. Most cruising sailboats of the time would have qualified.

When it came to aids to navigation, there weren't many. The North Americans were familiar with loran, the forerunner to today's Global Positioning System (GPS) technology. Loran, which is an acronym for long-range navigation, used the time interval between radio signals received from three or more stations to determine a boat's position. This information was displayed as latitude and longitude, which the navigator could transfer to a chart to pinpoint his location. Notoriously unreliable, especially in bad weather with low cloud cover, Loran was not allowed under Admiral's Cup rules. It was seen as an unfair advantage and the systems had to be disabled.

The only other electronic aid to navigation was a radio direction finder, a device that was aimed at the shore in the direction of a tower. The signal that came back gave a bearing and with two or three a skipper could plot his position. It was difficult to use in a storm and far from shore it was of no use at all. During that part of the race, navigation would be done by dead reckoning and plotting estimated position, based on average speed, currents, and tidal flow – what the purists called "proper navigation."

While *Pachena*'s skipper, John Newton, attended the final briefing, the crew went over the boat's gear, deciding what to take and what to leave behind. Weight was a big consideration. In 1979, boats didn't go to the extremes that racing sailboats do today, but the dockside decisions were the same. There wasn't much space below on *Evergreen*, and on *Magistri* all the comforts had been removed. She hadn't been painted inside to save eleven pounds' weight. The small marine toilet was positioned in the middle of the cabin to keep its weight centred. There were pipe berths for sleeping, a crude galley with an alcohol stove, and sails stashed everywhere. *Pachena* was the Cadillac of the bunch, with refrigeration and an enclosed head, but even her comforts were modest.

The toughest decision for all the crews was which sails to take. Each boat might have three or four spinnakers of differing weights of fabric and three or four jibs of varying sizes, including a storm jib, the smallest of the lot and designed for the worst weather. If the mainsails were reduced to the third reefs and the storm jib was up, the boat could sail safely in winds up to forty knots or more, managing gusts that might touch fifty. None of the Canadian boats was equipped with the sail of last resort, a storm trysail, which can be hoisted in place of the main in those rare survival conditions that nobody likes to contemplate.

On *Pachena*, the prevailing view was that they had done worse than expected in the races so far, partly because the boat was old and partly because the conditions were ones in which *Pachena* performed poorly. Steve Tupper, one of the most seasoned members of the team, felt *Pachena*'s crew was always having to struggle, even though it was performing at a high level. Tupper had sailed with her skipper, John Newton, for years, was the coach of Canada's national sailing team, and in his one trip to the Olympics in 1968 had come fourth in the Dragon class. He was one of the few Canadians who had been at the Admiral's Cup before, having sailed as a member of the first Canadian team to compete in 1975.

"We were outclassed and that was how it was," Tupper says. Like the other boats, *Pachena* wasn't used to losing. She was a perennial winner, the top boat in Vancouver, and a regular in the major races along the West Coast of the United States and Canada. John Newton liked victory and had a hundred or so trophies lining the wall of his West Vancouver home to prove it. But the Admiral's Cup had proven that *Pachena* was too old. The more modern designs,

*Pachena*'s crew at Cowes. From top left: Stewart Jones, John Simonett, Doug Race, Mike Schnetzler, Don Martin, Pat Leslie, Steve Tupper, Glenn Shugg, John Newton. (*Boudina Jones*)

with their broader sterns, surfed faster downwind and could gain a boat length on every wave. *Pachena* placed in the forties in a field of fifty-seven. When she came twenty-fourth in one of the races, it felt like first place to her crew. The youngest member, Stewart Jones, says, "We had a great party that night."

Still, the crew was eager for the last race. "We knew we weren't going to be in it, but damn it all, it was still good sailing, still a good experience, and we didn't stop trying," says John Simonett, who had missed representing Canada at the 1972 Olympics by a whisker, coming third in trials in which only the first and second places qualified.

*Pachena* had been shipped to England by freighter, reassembled, and fine-tuned in the Groves & Gutteridge yard at Cowes. Like Don Green, Newton had deep pockets, a voracious appetite for competition whether in rugby, business, or sailing, an enormous desire to win, and he indulged himself with a new boat every few years to further that cause. His experience included winter racing in Florida, plenty of Swiftsures – sometimes called the Driftsure – the big annual event in Victoria, and he always looked forward to the St. Francis Big Boat series in San Francisco, where twice he finished in third place overall. He had also raced for the Kenwood Cup, another West Coast favourite, run by the Royal Hawaiian Ocean Racing Club in Honolulu.

Newton is a tall, big-boned man whose Canadian roots go back to 1741. One of his ancestors fought on the Plains of Abraham in 1759 when Wolfe defeated Montcalm, ending French rule in Canada. His father was a research pathologist at the University of British Columbia. An uncle was president of the University of Alberta for twenty-three years. Another uncle was dean of the agriculture faculty at U of A. By 1979, Newton was the owner of Fletcher's Fine Foods, a meat-packing company in Vancouver, and rental properties in Vancouver and Toronto.

Newton loves all things nautical and has amassed a collection of 130 ship's journals from vessels involved in the exploration of the Pacific Northwest. They include the handwritten logs of captains Cook and Vancouver, and Vancouver's original charts of the B.C. coast printed in 1787.

Newton's boat, the four-year-old, forty-foot aluminum-hulled sloop *Pachena*, was designed by Doug Peterson of San Diego. She was painted white and, like all of Newton's sailboats, was called *Pachena* after Pachena Light on the west coast of Vancouver Island. At the end of the Second World War, when Newton was fifteen, he landed a job resupplying lighthouses and repainting buoys along the B.C. coast. The job took him to all sorts of isolated places, including the Pachena Light. "It is the most beautiful place, a gorgeous place, and so I've always called my boats *Pachena*," he says.

This *Pachena* had a flush deck, which meant plenty of room for the crew to move around. It had a small cabin, was fairly fat, and had the high stern typical of its time. It sailed well upwind but had a tendency to wobble going downwind. In West Coast races, it had not done as well in strong winds as it had in moderate to light air. She weighed eighteen thousand pounds, of which eight thousand pounds was the keel – overall, she was about 10 per cent lighter than *Magistri* but still 20 per cent heavier than *Evergreen*. She was pretty much obsolete by the time the first Admiral's Cup gun fired.

It had cost Newton almost $200,000 to buy the boat and $100,000 more to equip it, get it to England, and run the race. In Vancouver, many thought Newton crazy to spend so much on something as whimsical as ocean racing, where victory might amount to a handshake and a little tin cup. But Newton was a player, passionate about his sport, and in the enviable position of being able to indulge himself. So he did. As he says, "There's nothing more wonderful than racing in the Solent."

In 1979, Newton was forty-nine and captain of the Canadian Admiral's Cup team. The antithesis of Don Green, Newton was very much on the inside of the sailing community, an establishment man, who sat on the board of the Canadian Yachting Association. Like Green, he is a gentleman and a kind man too. During the Admiral's Cup races, he and Green became friends. They had a lot in common: success in business, pride in their achievements, and similar views of team building, leadership, and goal setting.

The two crews shared a bed and breakfast that former British prime minister Ted Heath had rented in a previous Admiral's Cup series and, it was said, where Anne Boleyn, Henry VIII's second wife, lived for a time. They ate breakfast together and then went their separate ways. Although the skippers and their wives socialized, the crews kept to themselves.

*Pachena*'s crew was experienced. They knew their boat and one another well. Some of them had been with Newton since he started offshore racing in the late 1960s. They had developed into a cohesive group, and they hoped to learn enough this time to come back and place well in 1981.

"I don't think we had any huge aspirations," said Don Martin, the starting helmsman. "We knew we weren't going to be front markers. That's not why we were there. We were there for an adventure."

The start of the race came during an uneasy truce with the weather. The tension among the crews was unbearable as the sailboats thundered with too much sail toward an imaginary starting line. On shore, hundreds of spectators sat in lawn chairs watching the spectacle unfold, their shouts of encouragement and warning lost in the wind. Aboard each boat, time seemed to slow as stopwatches ticked down the seconds. The crews' movements were measured and calmly precise, perfected by the repetition during all the races that had led to this day. Many of the sailors were filled with an exhilaration bordering on euphoria, even as they felt a familiar tightness in their stomachs.

This was it. This was why they had come to Cowes. This was the beginning of days of real reckoning, with legends pitted against novices, all racing in the world's fastest, sleekest boats. They had trained long and hard in all kinds of weather and were about to put it all on the line in a few long days that they knew could be wet, cold, and leave them exhausted to the point of collapse. That was part of the appeal.

Sharply at 1:30 p.m., at the Royal Yacht Squadron's signal, a cannon fired and the smallest boats in the fleet started, *Magic* among them. The gun fired every ten minutes for the next hour, the last to start being the so-called maxi boats, including Californian Jim Kilroy's seventy-nine-footer *Kialoa* and the seventy-seven-foot British-owned *Condor of Bermuda*.

At first the boats in each group were so close together the crews could reach out and shake hands – tons of shiny, flexing wood, fibreglass, aluminum, and steel slicing through the water just inches away from collision. But everybody knew the rules and assumed the other guy did too, so nobody gave an inch. There was a cacophony of men shouting, winches rasping, sails slapping. All sailing races start this way, but the Fastnet start was overwhelming because there were so many boats in a very small space, crewed by the most competitive people in the world, none of whom were giving any quarter.

There were sailors from twenty-two countries in North and South America, Europe, and Australasia, although 75 per cent were British or French. Irish entries made up 5 per cent, as did the Canadian and Americans combined. Sixty per cent of the fleet was boats that were thirty-eight feet or smaller. The Admiral's Cup boats were, for the most part, the largest, and made up about 20 per cent of the fleet.

A light-to-moderate westerly faded soon after the start, and the ebbing tide carried the fleet westward past the Needles, the western tip of the Isle of Wight, and into the English Channel. Among the Admiral's Cup boats, the Irish team was leading the series, to the surprise of the others. They were followed by the United States, Australia, and Hong Kong, whose sailors were all Britons with dual citizenship.

The start of the Admiral's Cup races was so crowded, at times
the sailors could touch the boat beside them. (*Sharon Green*)

The Canadian boats were in the fourth group to start. At 1:45 p.m., the three boats thundered down the line with the others. A large boat behind *Evergreen* ran aground and was stuck for hours. *Kialoa* and *Condor* moved through the group in a race of their own. Once past the Needles, all the skippers had to decide whether to head offshore or hug the rocky coast. Offshore meant lighter wind, a longer course, and the prospect of a collision with a freighter. Inshore meant land breezes, but strong tidal rips. *Evergreen* and *Pachena* stayed in, *Magistri* went out.

That evening, the inshore boats were trapped at Portland Bill, a finger of land that pokes out into the Channel, about forty miles west of the Isle of Wight. The fleet arrived at dusk and at the wrong end of a strong tide. Even though there was a good breeze, the current carried the boats toward the Bill. The boats would hug the beach, gather speed, and try to round the point, only to be swept back to the end of the line. The next boat would try and the next. Some, including *Evergreen*, dropped anchor to keep their position. The wind filling the sails made it appear that the boats were moving when, in fact, they were standing still.

Adding to the sense of the absurd was that the shore was lined with cars, their headlights shining out into the bay. The locals knew this biannual spectacle was not to be missed. *Evergreen* almost made it on her first attempt. On her second, she tucked in behind a larger Australian boat and followed him around, not just once but several times. An hour and a half later, the Australians got through.

Offshore, *Magistri's* crew found the conditions to their liking. The light breeze was a pleasant respite and everybody was relaxed. That evening, a chilling fog rolled in, and by midday Sunday, off Plymouth's Eddystone Lighthouse, about 120 miles down the course, the boat was creeping slowly along.

Nick DeGrazia heard the sound of an engine and the thumping of a propeller in the fog. DeGrazia, the only American on board *Magistri*, was the dean of graduate studies at the University of Detroit. He had never owned a boat but raced with other people on theirs. Because he was very skilled, he never lacked for a ride. He had hooked up with the others during a series on Lake Huron. They clicked, so he was invited back. DeGrazia knew by the sound that the boat was a freighter and was slightly ahead, but how close or at what angle – parallel or on collision course – he could not tell. The sound grew louder and the crew peered into the fog, wondering when and where the freighter would emerge. When it did, DeGrazia says, it was so close "you could have thrown a beer can and hit it. We were going to nail this thing broadside. Fred went to tack and Chuck Bentley screamed, 'No! Gybe.' We were that close."

# 4

# *Monday Morning*

**"If a man does his best, what else is there?"**

– U.S. GENERAL GEORGE S. PATTON

By EARLY MONDAY morning, the fleet had rounded Land's End, the westernmost point of Britain's south coast, and was heading northwest. The winds were still light, and most boats were drifting with their biggest spinnakers aloft. It was a welcome respite after two weeks of intense sailing, the likes of which most of the Canadians had never experienced before.

Most of the Admiral's Cup races in the previous two weeks had taken place in high winds and a steep chop. It blew most days, and then blew some more, the howling winds building short, steep seas and inflicting casualties on people, boats, and equipment. Brief periods of light breezes only accentuated how windy it was. Very strange conditions, considering how pleasant and settled a summer it had been. The forecast would call for moderate winds, but moderate would turn out to be anywhere between twenty and forty knots. Fred Goode says, "I remember thinking, Holy shit, what do they call it when it really blows?"

Goode had a strategic eye for the field and a steady hand at the helm, which is why he was usually the *Magistri* crew's choice to steer at the start. He could make sense of the chaos, where the aim is to cross the starting line just as the gun is fired and pull quickly ahead of the pack. A few seconds early and you were disqualified and forced to turn around and start again, effectively ending any chance of finishing well. A few seconds late and you were stuck in the crowd.

Goode had started hundreds of times in some pretty tough conditions and against some pretty savvy opponents, but in this series he was up against a competitive field unlike any he had ever known. "I was praying for someone else to take the start," Goode says. "I thought, Fred, this is definitely the big time."

As the boats tuned up, they kept waiting for familiar Great Lakes weather – a few days of screamers followed by light breezes. It didn't happen; the wind kept blowing. There was nothing they could do except buckle down and assume that because the kids at the local sailing school were dinghy racing in twenty-five knots it must be okay. Not only okay, but the way it always was.

"We didn't know any better," Bentley says.

At the upper end of the conditions, with winds in the thirty- to forty-knot range, small-boat races on the Great Lakes would be postponed. But in the English Channel, the Australians and Britons were licking their chops; heavy-weather sailing was their thing.

The Canadians had spent their first week in Cowes practising with other teams. Chuck Bentley was relentless in pushing *Magistri*'s crew to practise, practise, practise. One morning, he shook them awake and shoved them out the door. It was blowing so hard, there were few others out on the water, just dismasted boats limping back to port, Peter Cowern says.

Fred Goode estimated that during one session it was blowing close to forty knots, which on land would have made it difficult to walk upright. With the boat barely under control, he reckoned that would be a good time to hoist a spinnaker, which takes three or four people working together to set. Goode figured that if they didn't try then, without the pressure of being in a race, they would never have the courage to do it in the middle of one.

"We had to know if the boat could take it," he says. "So we popped the chute and the boat shook for ten minutes. We looked at one another and finally I said, 'Okay, that's enough,' and then we took it down.'" *Evergreen's* keel found one of the many unmarked rocks in the Solent while tuning up with some American boats. With Tim Stearn at the helm, she ventured too close inshore, heeled over on her side with too much of her retractable keel down. When she straightened up to tack, the keel smashed onto a rock and the boat stopped dead. The impact split the fibreglass sheath covering the keel and bent the aluminum frame, twisting it so badly the keel couldn't move.

When Rob Ball felt her smack into the rock, he believed *Evergreen's* Admiral's Cup adventure was over then and there. Ball had designed *Evergreen* and had come to England as part of the shore crew. *Evergreen* was the highlight of his career because she was so different, so innovative, and so fast. Ball had grown up in Port Credit, Ontario, but studied naval architecture at the University of Michigan. He was lucky enough to knock on C&C's door in 1969 just as it was expanding, and by 1973 he was chief designer. Ball stayed for twenty years and C&C's boats bear his distinctive stamp.

The keel had been the most challenging part, and now, with forty-eight hours to the start of the series, it was shattered.

In the fall of 1976, when Chuck Bentley was in Racine wondering whether to buy *Marauder*, Don Green approached C&C Yachts with a rare proposition. He wanted a boat whose only purpose was to win the Canada's Cup. The boat did not have to be a conventional design or built from traditional materials. It just had to win. What Green got was a boat that was so different those who saw it in action either liked it or hated it, there was no in-between. Author Douglas Hunter wrote in *Against the Odds*, the story of the *Evergreen*'s Canada's Cup campaign, that the boat was so radical it aroused "the disdain of critics and the fascination of onlookers more than any other yacht of her generation."

*Evergreen* looked very much like today's racing sailboats, which is why she looked so out of place when she was launched with wet snow falling in early November 1977. She slid into the water at Bronte Harbour in Oakville, Ontario, and after christening her with a bottle of champagne, everyone went inside to warm up. It wasn't until the next day that Green and her crew, wearing ski jackets, toques, and insulated gloves, took her out for a spin.

She was just over forty-one feet long, pointy at the front, flaring out to a width of fourteen feet, and then tapering slightly to the stern, which was flat on the waterline. The back of the boat was entirely open, so there was no need for cockpit drains. Other boats had deep cockpits where the crew could sit and brace themselves, but *Evergreen*'s was shallow and scalloped with plenty of room to move around. The disadvantage of this design was that there wasn't much to hang on to and no protection from breaking waves. But

From behind, *Pachena* and *Evergreen* looked like completely different
boats, with *Evergreen*'s innovative stern design contrasting with
*Pachena*'s traditional lines. (*Boudina Jones*)

her designers had figured that in Great Lakes match racing, there
were few breaking waves, and if large waves did break over the boat,
they would wash out the back. Skeptics wondered whether in conditions like that the crew might be washed away too, but for the
moment they kept those thoughts to themselves.

*Evergreen* weighed less than fifteen thousand pounds, compared
to *Magistri*'s twenty thousand pounds. The keel was an aluminum
frame covered in fibreglass with a 750-pound lump of lead at the
bottom. Another 8,750 pounds of lead was moulded into a rectan-
gular pancake fixed under her hull where the keel protruded into
the water. She drew eight feet with the keel fully down and less
than two feet fully up.

One of the boat's weaknesses was her instability with the keel
up. There wasn't enough weight below the water to counteract the

wind's force on the sails. The boat would wobble on the verge of broaching and had a disturbing tendency to skid sideways as if she was a skipping stone.

There were plenty of comments about what she looked like down below, most of which were murmurs of sympathy for the crew. The living space looked like the inside of an aircraft wing. Anywhere that plywood might have been used, panels made of fibreglass sandwiched over an aluminum honeycomb were substituted. The material was half the weight of mahogany ply and stiffer.

Most boats are strengthened by struts, or bulkheads, that span the boat, but *Evergreen* had aluminum trusses, which looked like the riveted struts of a Bailey bridge, running the length of the boat below decks on either side. They stiffened her so she wouldn't bend when the backstay was tensioned. The backstay is a wire that runs from the top of the mast to the back of the boat and can be tightened or loosened to adjust the bend of the mast and the shape of the sails.

The struts meant it was difficult to get into the sleeping berths, which looked like hinged stretchers just over two feet wide. You had to squeeze between the struts and the bulkhead and lie on your side, using a system of pulleys to loosen and tighten lines to keep the berth flat. The good news was that it was hard to fall out. There was a small marine toilet forward of the mast, but, like *Magistri*'s arrangement, it wasn't curtained off. As Steve Killing puts it, "We were all chums, after all."

The galley consisted of a panel of the aircraft material with a fifteen-inch hole fitted with a plastic bucket. That was the sink. There was no drain – you threw the contents overboard when it was full. There was an alcohol camping stove with a small oven, but there was no refrigeration. Dennis Aggus would make meals ashore, divide them into individual portions, and freeze them. They were put into a cooler where they gradually thawed. Once thawed, they were reheated.

In most boats, the way into the cabin is through a sliding hatch at the front of the cockpit. On *Evergreen*, it was through two hatches on either side of the mast. The thinking was that on a racing boat there are frequent sail changes, so the best place for a hatch is where sail changes take place. Designed as no-handed hatches, they opened downward on a spring-loaded hinge when kicked. It seemed a good idea, but during heavy weather in Florida in the winter of 1978, someone forgot to lock the hatch, or it was knocked open. The force of water rushing in nearly sank the boat. The hatches were replaced with traditional hatches that opened outward in time for the Admiral's Cup.

In the centre of the cockpit was a hydraulics console. A hand pump created pressure, and eight switches channelled the pressure to the various systems. The console was surrounded by an aluminum frame, which proved handy for the crew to hang on to. The hydraulics could quickly make adjustments to the tension on the backstay and forestay. It also controlled the boom vang, a metal extrusion like a shock absorber that keeps the boom at right angles to the mast and parallel to the deck. Hydraulics also raised and lowered the keel.

Among the names considered for the boat were *Green Machine* and *Green Light*. In the end, the consensus was for *Evergreen*, which stands for nothing in particular but connotes the North. After the launch, *Evergreen* was trucked down to Miami for a winter in the SORC, and overall her performance was a disappointment. She wasn't as fast as expected, and she certainly didn't look like a winner. The boat turned a lot of heads and Green didn't lack for advice. In the end, he decided it was back to the drawing board, with six months to go before the Canada's Cup.

Rob Ball says the answer came when John Bertram, the Australian America's Cup sailor, gave Ball his impressions of the boat. Bertram crewed on *Evergreen* for one race to check her out and told Ball that as boats got lighter, they had to get more pointy to compensate for the lack of weight to punch through waves.

"A light went on," Ball says. "I went back to the boat, took a chainsaw, cut open the bow, spread it apart, lengthened the water-line, and made it a sharp, pointy boat. That transformed *Evergreen* overnight."

*Evergreen* was often called a "rule beater" because she had been designed with a daggerboard keel to take advantage of the racing rules of the day. The rules said that boats with daggerboards were cruising boats, so they were allowed an extra eighteen inches of keel depth. This feature gave *Evergreen* an enormous advantage. When sailing upwind, the deeper the keel, the faster you go. Sailing down-wind, you want as little surface below water as possible, so you raise the keel. Green figured a rule was a rule and that his boat was legal and innovative.

*Evergreen* still looked odd, but her crew had reason for their high hopes as they stepped off the ferry in Cowes.

In the days before her keel smashed onto the rock, *Evergreen's* shore team had been working on something to protect the keel, but it was too late now. On the day of the accident, Tim Stearn had been steering. Given that it was a warm-up, most people would have steered a conservative course. "You don't push a race car in the practice as much as you would in the real race," Ball says. "But that message didn't get through to Timmy. He was a hell-bent-for-leather type of guy and couldn't differentiate between the two."

*Evergreen*'s crew remove her damaged keel for repairs after an accident in the Solent during the Admiral's Cup.

Awaiting the verdict on *Evergreen*'s keel. From left: Rob Ball (in hat), Al Megarry, Don Green, Jim Talmage, Dave Downey, and Dennis Aggus. (*Steve Killing*)

The crew managed to get *Evergreen* off the rock and limp back to the Groves & Gutteridge yard. The keel was bent so badly the only way to get it out was to drop the boat on the keel, so that the weight of the boat forced the keel up. Two days and a night later, *Evergreen* had a new keel that could no longer move. It was pinned in place but was probably not watertight. The shore crew had found an iron monger working out of a shed, and he had welded sheets of cold rolled steel to the old frame. A sailing journalist called the repairs "strong, but crude."

When Ball looked at the new keel, he figured it added between two hundred and four hundred pounds to the boat. The weight didn't hurt so much now because the boat was racing in high winds, but the sharp, welded edges, compared with the curves of the original keel, were another matter.

"It wasn't the same boat," Ball says.

In the second warm-up race, *Pachena* broke her mast. The lower spreader, a support used to guide the shrouds from the top of the mast to the deck, sheered where it attached to the mast. The crew had been putting more and more bend into the mast by tightening the backstay. In strong wind, adding bend lets you flatten the sail so you can travel at a closer angle to the wind. But *Pachena's* mast wasn't built to be bent. She flew over a wave, and the mast moved every so slightly. There was enough play that when she landed, the spreader broke, and with the tension unbalanced on the remaining shrouds, the mast shattered about ten feet from the top. Doug Race shimmied up and it was the better part of an hour later before the tangle of rigging was carefully removed and the mainsail lowered intact. The dispirited crew wondered how they were going to fix it with just a day and a half to the start of the Cup. Then Tim Stearn from *Evergreen* tracked down a mast blank in a Lymington boatyard, and the crew transferred all the old hardware.

One of the casualties
of the Admiral's Cup
was *Pachena*'s mast.
(*Sharon Green*)

"We were lucky to get it," Don Martin says. "But talk about opportunism. Boy, that was probably the most expensive piece of aluminum tubing ever sold."

It wasn't an exact fit, but what could they do? It would probably hold together, but the question was how much would it take in a blow. One never knew the answer to that until it happened.

The teams regrouped after their battering in the warm-ups. They were chastened but still optimistic, wondering about the first

The Argentine boat *Madrugada* at the Groves & Gutteridge yard after
her collision at the start of the first Admiral's Cup race. (*Ann Bobyk*)

real deal, the thirty-mile inshore race in the Solent. As they made
their way out of the harbour to the start, there were the same fitful
gusts and angry grey skies, the wind light one moment and then
gusting to twenty-five and thirty knots the next.

For the Argentine and Brazilian boats, things went quickly and
horribly wrong just a few minutes before the start of the race.
*Madrugada* from Argentina had the right of way, but *Sur II* from
Brazil refused to budge. When they collided, the impact drove *Sur's*
pointed bow through the side of *Madrugada's* hull like a harpoon,
peeling her flank open from the deck to the waterline and threatening to sink her on the spot. Her crew hurriedly dropped sails and
moved to the opposite side of the boat, where they climbed out
onto a spinnaker pole, using their weight and the pole as a fulcrum

to keep the boat upright and to stop water from rushing in. *Madrugada* limped to shore, but the Cup was over for her, before the series had even begun.

These races offered yet another humbling lesson, because they involved tactics the Canadians had heard about but had never tried. The races were won or lost by driving your boat straight into shore, as if you planned to beach it, and at the last minute tacking back out into the Channel. The boats hugged the shore because farther out, the current was so strong that at full tide it could run as much as nine knots against you. The prevailing wisdom was that it was acceptable to run aground near the shore five or six times in a race, as long as you could get unstuck within ten seconds or so.

The first leg of most sailing races is upwind, and since sailboats can't go directly into the wind, they must zigzag. All fifty-seven boats, just feet apart, would be moving in a pack, on one tack, then the other. It could be tricky when they headed into shore.

Sweaty-palmed skippers, with one hand on the tiller and an eye on their depth sounders, would wait until there was about a foot or so of water left under the keel before they turned. The last boat in the line would be pinned, unable to tack until the boat beside his did, and so on up the line. Some skippers would panic and shout for room to manoeuvre. The lead boat would wait as long as possible, hoping to cause some other boat to shipwreck or at least run aground, and at the last moment tack. The rest of the fleet would follow in synchronization.

"The tactics were something I had never seen before," says Nick DeGrazia. "The last guy in the line is screaming, and pretty soon everyone is screaming."

This game of chicken was played out many times. The slightest misjudgment, or lack of nerve, could lead to catastrophe. This part of the race required enormous stamina and strength to tighten, trim, release, and trim the sails again, over and over. "Guys were puking their guts out in the first mile," Fred Goode says. "We realized we had to get in shape because this was standard."

The real eyeopener was the start. The line stretched for a mile, but one end was favoured because it had the least current. This was the end that was so close to the clubhouse you could toss a chocolate bar to someone standing on the deck. It was appropriately nicknamed Wrinkle City, as boats collided, fended one another off, and everyone cursed and swore with the vigour and colour of half a dozen languages.

There were times on the start line when Ron Barr was so unnerved he didn't want to know what was going on.

Barr had sailed with Don Green for several years and at one point had been Green's crew boss for Wednesday-night club racing. It was his job to round up people for the boat and make sure they showed up, tasks that suited Barr's personality. He was a high-school teacher and enjoyed being the leader and organizer. He usually had an opinion and liked to express it.

When Barr got mad, you knew it, though he was not one to hold a grudge. He was angriest at his own mistakes, and the scowl that made his bushy eyebrows twitch often led to a self-deprecating laugh. He liked difficult tasks, was energized by competition, and was always willing to work hard.

Barr had long dreamed of big-league sailing, either the America's Cup or the Olympics. Both had passed him by earlier, but now, despite the starting-line horrors, he was competing against the best in the world and that made him a happy man. If he'd had to, he would have walked bare foot over broken glass to get to this starting line. Even so, he says, "I kept my head down and looked at the winches, because I didn't want to see what was happening."

In one race, *Magistri* lured a boat to disaster. It was well known

The Admiral's Cup races attracted huge crowds
to the seafront at Cowes. (*Arch Alyea*)

that *Magistri*'s seven-and-a-half-foot keel was one of the deeper ones. Other boats reckoned that if she was close to shore, sailing on her outside was safe. *Magistri*'s navigator, John Hollidge, made a swift calculation based on the tide tables, current flow, and time of day and figured she could pass through a narrow channel between shore and the Gerrard Ledge, a submerged shelf of rock a few hundred yards offshore. *Magistri* made it through the channel with maybe a foot to spare, but the unsuspecting boat following her wasn't paying attention and drove onto the ledge. The impact drove the boat out of the water as its keel rode up the rocks.

"Did they stop? Boy, did they ever," Hollidge says. "Very quickly."

This kind of action made the Admiral's Cup races a great spectator sport, and like the crowds in the Roman Coliseum, the visitors came to be entertained. They would sit in their chairs with a blanket covering their laps, binoculars in hand, and watch the fun.

They cheered when boats ran aground and laughed as the crews tried to refloat them.

"It was priceless," says Don Green. It wasn't simply a matter of getting a good start. The fleet had to dodge hundreds of non-racing sailboats of all sizes, the press launches, spectator boats, and even for a while the royal yacht *Britannia*, anchored off the entrance to Cowes Harbour. One start was delayed for twenty minutes to allow a freighter to pass through the course.

At the end of the first race, *Evergreen* was thirty-seventh, *Magistri* forty-first, and *Pachena* forty-eighth, putting Canada eighteenth of the nineteen competing countries, a few points ahead of Poland.

In the second inshore race the following day, a British boat, *Inishanier*, was rounding a mark when a gust of wind knocked her over. Her mast touched the water, then she popped up and, like a pendulum, swung over to the other side in a crash gybe. The boom was flung across the boat, cracking a crewman on the head. He crumpled on deck, bleeding profusely. The skipper radioed for help, and the man was soon lowered into a nearby press boat, from where a Royal Navy helicopter airlifted him to hospital. He fully recovered. Soon afterwards, the Japanese boat *Togo VI* was sailing full tilt downwind when her skipper lost control, the boat broached, the boom swung and knocked a crewman out cold. He, too, was evacuated and, four stitches to his scalp later, pronounced fully recovered. During the same race, Fred Goode looked over his shoulder to see *Evergreen* rolling heavily and then go right over as her crew hung on for dear life.

"She took forever to right," says Goode. "I wondered, How long before she sinks?"

In the second race, the Canadian team did worse. *Evergreen* placed forty-sixth, *Magistri* forty-seventh, and *Pachena* fifty-second.

The rivalry between the Toronto and Hamilton boats contin-ued where it had left off in the Canada's Cup. Chuck Bentley was so steamed when *Evergreen* refused to yield the right of way on one occasion, he threatened to launch a protest and let the race committee adjudicate. When John Newton pointed out that it would look odd if one Canadian boat team protested another, Bentley relented.

It became clear that *Evergreen* was too light and difficult to handle in very windy conditions. Racing downwind, she was on the verge of broaching all the time. On the Great Lakes, races have long legs, which give each crew plenty of time to tweak their boat to make it go faster and catch up to the guy in front. On *Evergreen*, with the boat doing exhausting tacks upwind and white-knuckle downwind legs, the crew couldn't move fast enough to make use of the many features that had previously made her a winner.

"The boat was just too gadgety," Dennis Aggus says. "In match racing, you make these adjustments at your leisure, change the shape of the sail, tune the mast, play, play, play, until you go faster. In the Solent, we didn't have time."

The modifications that were made to the boat before she was shipped to England were also proving to be a problem. That winter, *Evergreen*'s mast had been shortened by about eighteen inches and some hydraulics systems had been removed to meet the Admiral's Cup rules. Weight had been added to her keel for the same reason. The changes made her that much slower. While *Pachena* and *Magistri* noted with satisfaction that they were keeping up with *Evergreen*, they weren't competing against the same boat as the year earlier.

"I knew going into the Cup we were in trouble," Jim Talmage says. "When we put the boat in the water that spring, we sailed a couple of races in Toronto and had trouble keeping up with guys we had sailed away from the previous year. It wasn't a pleasant experience."

"We thought we'd kick ass, but the competition blew us away," Talmage says. "That was a rude awakening."

*Evergreen* wasn't alone in having a rough time. During the series, a Belgian skipper died of a heart attack. On another Belgian boat, a crewman's foot became tangled in a loose line, and he was dragged along the length of his boat and knocked unconscious. In the cross-Channel race to Cherbourg, Ted Heath's forty-four-footer *Morning Cloud* broke her rudder – and that was in the lightest wind of the series. In this race, the Canadians did better. *Pachena* came in twenty-fourth, *Evergreen* thirty-fourth, and *Magistri* thirty-sixth.

After a hard day on the course, the one challenge left was getting safely into the yacht club. The moorings were surrounded by a concrete seawall with an opening about thirty feet wide. The current ran across the entrance so each helmsman had to drive at full throttle upwind of the entrance, knowing that if he misjudged the current he could drive his boat into the breakwater and sink it. The hope was that by aiming high the boat would be carried down into the opening, where throwing the engine into full reverse would prevent the boat from ramming into the wall dead ahead. For those already safely tied up, it was a source of great amusement to watch the boats come in.

"We came through after one race and, Jesus, the boat wouldn't go in reverse," Goode says. "I'm thinking, This is not good, there's a cement wall ahead of me. Finally, I got it into neutral, but we're still moving too fast. I see an open slip about four or five boat lengths ahead, so I swing into that, get the boat into reverse at the last minute, open the engine up, and the boat stops. Of course, everyone is standing up and clapping, and the sweat is rolling off my forehead."

The boat behind them wasn't so lucky. The skipper also couldn't find reverse fast enough and hit the wall a glancing blow at about five knots.

# 5

# The Irish Sea

*"Once you eliminate the impossible, whatever remains,
no matter how improbable, must be the truth."*

— SHERLOCK HOLMES

AT THE START of the third day of the Fastnet race, life on board
*Pachena* was good after the pace of the past two weeks. Don Martin
was enjoying the light air, it was West Coast weather. Martin had
grown up in Vancouver and was a long-time member of the Royal
Vancouver Yacht Club. He had tinkered with boat building from
the age of twelve and, after graduating from the University of
British Columbia with an architecture degree, had set up shop on
his own. He had already designed a twenty-nine-foot cruising sailboat and was soon to launch the Martin 24, which became widely
popular on the West Coast.

"We were happy the Fastnet was turning into a moderate race,"
he says. "It was a third of the way through, and we were doing all
right. There was a bit of uncertainty about the weather. Something
might be coming, but that was only a possibility."

A few miles offshore, between Land's End and the Scilly Isles, *Evergreen* came across mackerel fishermen in twenty-foot wooden skiffs, eager to sell her their catch. It hardly seemed like a boat race at all. The boat was moving at about three to five knots. Don Green chatted with them and felt disquieted when they predicted that the mild conditions wouldn't last, that the winds were going to increase, and there was a storm coming. There was no word of that on the BBC weather service.

On board, Dave Downey was down for the count. Downey had been part of the team since the Canada's Cup days and was a great sailor but was susceptible to motion sickness. He was in England as part of the shore crew, responsible for maintaining *Evergreen* and fixing things that broke. At the last minute, he was asked to help sail *Evergreen*. Because he was prone to seasickness, before he left Hamilton, a doctor gave him something to help. "It was a combination of uppers and downers," Steve Killing says. "I don't know how much he remembers, but he was sleeping most of the time. After the first night, he went down to sleep and didn't come up until the storm was over."

Most people have motion sickness to one extent or another. Some feel slight nausea and can still work, but others become so ill they think they're dying and hope someone will put them out of their misery. Most astronauts get motion sickness because they float weightless and the normal cues the brain needs to interpret where it is are not there. Many people taking their first helicopter trip are also affected, because the eyes tell the brain that the body is floating in space, while muscles and spine receptors tell the brain the body is sitting down.

Many people feel more seasick down below than on deck. Down below, the eyes are telling the brain everything is normal, while muscle receptors are detecting an up-and-down motion. On deck, the eyes, ears, and receptors are all receiving the same message – extreme movement, with the eyes watching the horizon. Once seasickness starts, it can't be stopped. It has to run its course. It sometimes takes days to get "sea legs."

The most common anti-nausea drugs are antihistamine-based. All of them leave you drowsy, which on a small boat in the open ocean is an invitation to disaster. So racing sailors often combine antihistamines with amphetamines to keep them awake. Fred Goode was prone to seasickness and would take both drugs before setting out on longer trips.

"We used to have a brown pill and a white pill," he says. "But you had to be careful, if you took two browns you'd be out for a couple of watches."

Gradually that Monday morning, visibility improved, but the ocean had an oily look; some later described it as glassy. There were small undulations, but no real waves, and the boats were barely making headway. The sun hid behind a haze and the sky had an ominous feel.

On *Magic*, Peter Whipp was fretting. He had a four-horsepower engine that was used to bring *Magic* in and out of harbour. It was down below, securely lashed. *Magic* also carried a portable generator to charge the batteries used to run the radio, cabin lights, and other electrical needs. Whipp turned it on to make sure the batteries were fully charged for the coming night. "I thought to myself, Tonight we're in for a rough one."

By midday, the Admiral's Cup boats were well into the Irish Sea, and Fastnet Rock was about 150 miles to the northwest. The wind had shifted from south to west-southwest, and the sailing was good as the big racing boats broad reached on a point of sail that favoured their billowing spinnakers. The lead boats, *Condor*, *Kialoa*, and Ted Turner's *Tenacious*, were already closing in on Fastnet. *Kialoa* rounded just before 1:00 p.m. and *Condor* a little after 2:00 p.m. At the other end of the race, some of the smaller boats were still trying to round Land's End.

*Kialoa's* maximum speed, based on her waterline length, was 11.9 knots, while *Evergreen's* was 8.6 knots, or about 30 per cent slower. *Magic* was 15 per cent slower than *Evergreen*. Each boat could go faster when surfing, but when sailing flat out in ideal conditions their hull speed was it. It made a difference over a long course such as the Fastnet. When the leading boats entered the Irish Sea, the laggards were already as much as eight hours behind, leaving the 303 boats stretched out in a long line in the relatively shallow water of the Western Approach to Britain.

*Magistri's* navigator, Lt. John Hollidge, was well into his routine by now, one he thoroughly enjoyed. Hollidge, a career Royal Navy officer, sat at the chart table hour after hour, using age-old tools to plot *Magistri's* position, taking into account tides and current and parsing the weather bulletins for information that might provide a tactical edge. Hollidge is a purist – he loves paper charts, dividers, and parallel rules, believing that navigation is an art that involves the accumulated skills of seafaring tradition. For him, loran, GPS, and other electronic aids, with their push-button displays of latitude and longitude, took all the fun out of sailing. "To me, that wasn't navigation," he says. "That wasn't ocean racing."

Many non-English Admiral's Cup boats offered places to sailors with knowledge of the Solent. The rocky shores there make the lack of local help an invitation to come last, or worse. The tidal streams are fast and there is a large rise and fall in the tide, up to four metres. You can sail over rocks in one hour that you'd run aground on an hour later.

As luck would have it, the twenty-nine-year-old Hollidge was at loose ends. His ship was in the middle of a refit, and since the Navy encouraged its officers to participate in ocean races, Hollidge was granted adventure leave. He had trained at the Royal Naval Engineering College in Plymouth and spent his summers cruising the coast of France, including the infamous Bay of Biscay, which he maintains is not that frightening a place. In 1975 and 1977, he raced in the Fastnet on boats that were in the middle to the top of the field.

Ian Craik, a Canadian friend of Bentley, had joined the Royal Navy, knew Hollidge, and approached him on their behalf. Craik was part of the shore crew, but did not sail, nor did another Toronto sailor, Paul Dickson. Hollidge wasn't sure if he wanted to race on a boat with six skippers, but when Bentley assured him that he was the boss, Hollidge agreed.

Until this point in the race, Hollidge hadn't been particularly impressed by the weather. "I suppose it's what you're used to," he says. "There were good winds, but I wouldn't call them particularly strong. It wasn't a blood-stained year at that point, if you know what I mean."

Every hour, he updated *Magistri*'s position on his chart, plotting her advance along the line drawn to the Fastnet. The boat had an instrument at the top of the mast that measured wind speed and direction and, if needed, Hollidge could drag out the radio direction finder and get a bearing from a shore-based radio tower to confirm his dead-reckoning position. Ever since rounding Land's End, the barometer had been falling. It was slow, but as the afternoon wore on the descent continued. A blow was coming, though how bad was hard to tell.

Hollidge's experience told him the wind would become more westerly when the storm arrived. If *Magistri* continued on her present course, the straight, or rhumb line, course, she would end up with the wind pretty close to dead ahead, meaning she would have to tack back and forth in the middle of the night to make forward progress. *Magistri* would be sailing two or three miles for every mile of forward progress, a slow, tiring process. The storm was bound to bring high wind and big seas to add to the fatigue that was always a factor in long-distance sailing. The more exhausted the crew, the fewer the hands available to work the boat; the fewer the hands, the faster they tired; the faster they tired, the greater the likelihood of a mistake.

Hollidge reasoned that if *Magistri* headed due west while she still could, although it was away from Fastnet, she could make the ground up later when the wind shifted to the northwest, which it would likely do once the storm passed. *Magistri* would be able to ease off and sail toward the rock, which would play to the boat's strengths. Hollidge laid out his plan for skipper Chuck Bentley. Bentley was unimpressed.

He remembers thinking: What does he know? But as the wind kept building and started to shift, Bentley changed his mind. "I thought, Maybe he's right, maybe he does know what he's talking about." He turned *Magistri* west, making a beeline for Newfoundland.

Nick DeGrazia's memories of Monday afternoon and early evening are a series of vignettes: a one-man play in which John Hollidge's lean, bearded face pokes up through the hatch to announce cheerfully that the barometer is still falling. "The first time John came on deck, he said, 'It looks like we're going to have some rain,'" DeGrazia says. "I thought, Okay, fine. Half an hour later, he pops up and says, 'Well, the barometer is still falling and so

I think we might get a little more than rain, maybe a thunderstorm.'
Okay, fine. Forty-five minutes later, he comes on deck and says,
'Well, the barometer is still falling and I must say, it is falling quite
rapidly, so we're going to have something worse than a thunderstorm, but I don't know what it is, but it's probably going to blow
like hell tonight.'" Hollidge had endured a typhoon in the Sea of
Japan the previous year while serving on HMS *Tiger* and knew that
the speed of this drop meant the approaching system was packing
a wallop.

"The last time he came up," DeGrazia says, "his comment was,
'I have never seen the barometer fall this far, this fast in all my years
at sea, and I have no idea what we're going to run into tonight.' But,
what are you going to do? You're umpteen miles offshore in the
Irish Sea. You have no place to go. So, we just kept going."

At about 3:00 p.m., according to position reports filed with the race
committee, *Pachena* was almost eight miles ahead of *Magistri*. Her
crew was making the same sort of strategic calculation, but instead
of going west, they decided to head north, or downwind. As the
boat changed course, her speed increased because the angle to the
wind was less acute and she could broad reach, a point of sail she
was built for. *Pachena* barrelled along at nine knots and sometimes
twelve knots as she surfed with her big spinnaker flying. The crew
knew they would be below their intended destination, but figured
they could make up the lost ground that evening.

Mike Schnetzler's job was to help with sail changes – setting
the spinnaker when a large light-wind sail was needed and changing down to progressively smaller sails when the wind piped up.
Schnetzler, thirty-two, was a mechanical engineering graduate

from the University of British Columbia and had known most of the crew for years, either from the local racing scene or university. John Simonett, the other engineer on board, had been a year ahead of him at UBC. Schnetzler had been part of the team for about ten years and was comfortable in the open ocean. What he found strange that afternoon was how it became progressively darker from lunch onward. There was a claustrophobically low cloud ceiling, which looked ominous against the glassy water. It felt as if all hell were going to break loose. The water became so dark, Schnetzler says it was like an ocean of ink. "I stuck my finger in and remember thinking, I wonder why this isn't coming up blue?" he says. "It was the funniest thing."

At the helm, Steve Tupper watched as the Australian boat *Impetuous* altered course and, as *Magistri* had done, headed west. Tupper wondered why. The Australians were ferocious competitors, so he figured they'd changed course for some tactical advantage, but he couldn't see what. Tupper talked it over with John Simonett, who didn't know what to make of it either, so they shrugged and carried on.

Simonett was another calm influence on board, a vastly experienced, rock-solid guy who could be counted on in the clutch. Simonett had worked his way up the sailing ladder in offshore races. He had caught Newton's eye and kept getting invited back.

A marine engineer, with a pilot's licence and a penchant for scuba diving in out-of-the-way places, Simonett gets pleasure from risky pursuits. "I don't bungee jump, put it that way, and I don't go looking for it," he says, "but I suppose I take some satisfaction in doing dangerous things safely."

The BBC's 1:55 p.m. marine forecast didn't offer any new information or cause for alarm. It still called for southwesterly Force 4 or Force 5 winds, increasing to Force 6 or Force 7 for a time, and then veering west later. There was a possibility of occasional rain or showers.

Force 4 on the Beaufort scale is a "moderate breeze" with winds between eleven and sixteen knots. Force 5 is a "fresh breeze" between seventeen and twenty-one knots. The lower end of Force 7, a "near gale," is twenty-eight knots and the upper end is thirty-three knots. That afternoon, the fleet was sailing in the lower end of Force 4, conditions that were ideal for the race. The forecast confirmed what had been known since Saturday's briefing: a storm was coming, but not with any more intensity than *Pachena*'s crew had experienced before. It would add spice to the second half of the race, something to talk about at the club when it was all over.

Much later, Tupper learned that one of the Australian crew spoke French and had picked up a French forecast. Its prediction was that around Fastnet Rock late Monday and early Tuesday, the upper end of the wind *could be* Force 8, a full gale, with a maximum speed of forty knots. "We didn't get to hear that, so we could see no reason to alter our course," Tupper says.

Something else had been bothering *Pachena*'s crew. The boat always seemed to be slightly off course. It hadn't been obvious during the inshore Admiral's Cup races that called for line-of-sight sailing, but during the cross-Channel race to France and back, the errors had been noticeable. The crew put it down to pilot error, even though their navigator, Pat Leslie, was an Air Canada pilot who knew his stuff inside and out and rarely made mistakes. Newton had weighed the pros and cons of hiring a local navigator, as Bentley and Green had done, but decided against it. Leslie was so skilled, Newton didn't think a local was necessary. The crew found it hard to believe he was making a mistake, but couldn't think what else it could be. They kept asking if the course was right, and Leslie would confirm that it was. Beyond a few muttered asides, nobody pressed the point. It was just one of those things.

Accident theory predicts that in a tightly coupled system – an environment where many things are connected – the smallest thing can lead to catastrophic failure. A racing sailboat is a very tightly coupled system, and while the failures of small things are not dangerous by themselves they can start a cascade of problems. In the 2002 Around Alone race, a single-handed around-the-world sailing race, a five-cent screw put American sailor Tim Kent's life in peril. The screw attached the grounding wire of his engine to the keel and came loose, causing the wire to come off. Kent was in the perilous Southern Ocean and believed he was charging his batteries when he ran the engine for a few hours each day. Instead, he was gradually draining them. When they were sufficiently discharged, his autopilot failed, and in twenty-five knots of wind, the boat gybed and broached. Kent was asleep down below and hurled across the cabin. He was alone in the most dangerous and inhospitable place on Earth, a thousand miles from land, without any power to run the instruments he depended upon for navigation, to communicate with the outside world, and heat his cabin in near-freezing temperatures.

Kent stopped the boat, took all sail down, and after some searching found the loose wire and reattached it. His boat had solar panels as a backup, so he shut everything down and waited. A few hours later, he had enough charge to start his engine, and he was on his way.

The real problem was that *Pachena*'s compass was off by a few degrees. This wasn't dangerous in and of itself. But when the compass course is off by ten or fifteen degrees in the middle of a storm, at night, barely in control, sailing on a course that takes the boat within a few miles of the Irish Coast, suddenly those ten degrees are vital. An inaccurate compass can be fatal.

Yale University sociology professor Charles Perrow concludes in *Normal Accidents*, his book about catastrophes and near-catastrophes in high-risk industries, that most calamities have small beginnings. The Big Bang usually starts with a small sigh. But often the error is caused not by negligence, but stems from a failure so unlikely that it is not considered as a source of the problem. It is only in hindsight that the cause is revealed. Before the accident, no one could know what was going on and what should have been done.

Pat Leslie was properly performing his tasks of estimating the boat's position and plotting a course. He was unable to diagnose the problem, because he was trying to solve the problem with an inaccurate tool. He was recalculating the course he'd plotted to make sure the numbers were right, and each time he ran the numbers he got the same answer. Nobody was looking at the possibility of compass error because they were focused on the "logical" explanation. *Pachena*'s compass was accurate before the boat arrived in England, so there was no reason to suspect it wasn't working now. But something was causing the deviation.

*Pachena* was an aluminum-hulled boat and left Vancouver with an aluminum propane tank stored in a cockpit locker, not far from the compass. Since it was aluminum, it would not have caused any compass error. But the tank had been changed.

Stewart Jones, a graduate student at Simon Fraser University, arrived in England before the rest of the crew since it was his job to rig the boat, check its systems, and maintain it during the series. Before the crew moved into the shared house with the *Evergreen* crew, Jones lived aboard and used the stove to cook. When the tank was empty, he couldn't find a dealer who would refill a North American propane tank. He discarded it and bought a new one and

Stewart Jones takes a break in *Pachena's* cockpit
before the start of the Fastnet race. (*Boudina Jones*)

put it back in the compartment. The replacement tank was steel,
and in all the excitement surrounding the Admiral's Cup, Jones
forgot about it and the compass was never adjusted for the mag-
netic deviation caused by its proximity to the tank. That was why
the compass was off by more than ten degrees. A small thing, but
potentially calamitous.

After Don Green's disquieting conversation with the fisherman
on Monday morning, *Evergreen's* navigator, Alan Jeyes, paid particular attention to the weather. Green's sense of unease hadn't left
him from the moment the fleet set sail, but there was nothing of
note in the BBC's 1:55 p.m. forecast so *Evergreen* had a pleasant afternoon. While *Magistri* had gone west and *Pachena* north, *Evergreen*
was sailing between both of them, on a northwest course, along the
straightest line to Fastnet Rock.

# 6

# Storm Warning

**"Fear is like fire. It can cook for you. It can heat your house. Or it can burn it down."**

– BOXING TRAINER CUS D'AMATO

*T*HE SIZE OF the approaching weather bomb was impressive. In his first-person account of the race, *Fastnet, Force 10*, John Rousmaniere describes it as a compact, violent storm whose uneven impact created "pockets of fury" over the fleet. It had travelled more than five thousand miles in four days and was poised to sweep across the Western Approaches during the hours when they would be crowded with small racing yachts.

The storm had formed in Minnesota at around the same time that *Magic* was in the English Channel, making her way to Cowes for the start of the race. It was among one of any number of storms that form and dissipate on the Great Plains during the summer, the product of hot, moist air colliding with cold air sweeping down from the north. This storm moved east, dropping an inch and a half of rain on Minneapolis late Thursday afternoon. The next day it developed into violent thunderstorms with hail in Wisconsin and northern Michigan before crossing Georgian Bay into southern Ontario. On Friday, twenty-four hours after the storm formed, two people died and 130 more were injured in Woodstock, a community near London, when the system spawned a tornado. Dozens of homes and farm buildings were destroyed. The storm then veered southeast, crossing Lake Ontario and blowing into Upstate New York. Power was knocked out in New York City, and the roof was blown off a tollbooth on the New Jersey Turnpike. In Newport, Rhode Island, where small-boat sailors were competing at the J24 Worlds, thirty-five knot winds flattened the fleet. The storm changed course again, veered north toward Nova Scotia, where it arrived on the day the Fastnet race started. Then it travelled out into the North Atlantic and faded.

By mid-afternoon Sunday, the system had moved about eight hundred miles east of Nova Scotia. By mid-afternoon Monday, when Steve Tupper noticed the Australian boat alter course to the west, it had moved roughly twelve hundred miles closer to the fleet. Had it continued to move due east, its centre would have been hundreds of miles to the south, somewhere in the middle of the Bay of Biscay, around Bordeaux, France. But it was hitching a ride on a warm front known as the Azores High, whose southwesterly winds were pushing the system northeast. This change in direction put it on a collision course with the fleet.

As the storm passed over Nova Scotia, another area of low pressure, stretching in a thousand-mile band from the southern tip of Greenland to the same latitude as Ireland, was moving slowly east. It had formed over Labrador and moved out to sea on Sunday, as the fleet was moving slowly west in the English Channel in the fog. This storm's centre was 350 miles southwest of Iceland. It kept moving, with high winds and rain, but then it, too, slowed down.

This allowed the first system to move ahead and push north. Some years later, author Sebastian Junger would coin the phrase *perfect storm* to describe the collision of two such powerful weather systems.

Weather systems spin as they move, and in the northern hemisphere they spin clockwise. The wind direction changes as a storm passes by. If you are on the north side of the storm when it overtakes you, the wind will blow from the northeast, hence the old sailing proverb that an east wind blows no good. If you are to the south of the storm, which the fleet was at first, the wind comes from the southwest. This was initially a favourable direction for the fleet, allowing it to move toward Fastnet. As the system passed by, the wind moved clockwise from southwest to west to northwest so quickly that enormous waves coming from the northwest direction were colliding with others that had built up during the southwesterly flow and had not had a chance to subside. These so-called confused seas come from several directions at once, without a predictable pattern. Fifty-foot waves and eighty-knot gusts would be typical, even though it normally takes days of consistent high winds from one direction to build waves of that size.

British forecasters were later criticized for not noticing the storm soon enough. Staff at the British Meteorological Office did see it, but with the tools they had at hand, they couldn't assess its severity. In 1979, most of the orbiting satellites were primarily for military use, with very little capacity turned over to civilian agencies. They did their best and realized by around noon Monday they had a little monster on their hands. The news arrived too late for the BBC's 1:55 p.m. broadcast.

The Met Office put out a special bulletin warning that a Force 8 gale was imminent over southern Ireland, including the Fastnet. *Imminent* meant within six hours. The BBC broke into its normal

Radio 4 broadcasting to issue the bulletin at intervals. But the fleet wasn't listening. They had been told to tune in precisely four times a day, and on many boats the radios were turned off to save battery power. For the Canadians and Americans, accustomed to continuous marine broadcasts, receiving just four forecasts a day was another quirk of Admiral's Cup racing.

The 5:50 p.m. broadcast brought more clarity, and it confirmed Don Green's worst fear. It was the news he had missed at midday: Force 8 at Fastnet – between thirty-four and forty knots – with the storm now centred about 250 miles west of the rock, or about 300 miles from *Evergreen*'s position. Just fifteen minutes later, the Met Office revised its estimate of the wind strength, calling for imminent Force 8 or 9. The upper end of Force 9 is forty-seven knots. Navigator Alan Jeyes heard the revision, although many in the fleet missed it and wouldn't hear the news until 12:15 a.m. By then, they would be struggling for their lives.

The North Americans had to do some mental math. They were more used to actual wind speeds than the Beaufort scale shorthand. Once they did the calculation, their pulses quickened. On land at Force 9, houses with slate roofs will lose tiles, trees sway and bend, and it is only possible to walk into the wind hunched over. At Force 10, just shy of a hurricane, trees can be uprooted and poorly constructed buildings will come down.

The fleet now was at its most vulnerable, stretching out the entire length of the relatively shallow Western Approach to Britain. *Evergreen* was finding it difficult to sail toward the Fastnet because, as the wind veered from southwest to west, the boat had to bear away from its course just to keep sailing. The sea was not uncomfortable, but the waves were rising, still with a long fetch. For now, the boat rode up and down them fairly easily. The wind speed was between twenty and twenty-five knots, and the *Evergreen* crew had long since lowered her spinnaker and big reaching genoa and was moving down in sail size.

"It was starting to get risky," Don Green says. "Anything we get over fifteen knots is risky, anything over twenty-five very risky. Anything above that is disastrous, because I don't think the boat will hold together."

Around 6:00 p.m., Ron Barr looked to the west, the direction of the approaching storm, and saw a strange greenish tinge around the sun. He had never seen its like before, and it made him anxious. At about the same time, about thirty miles to the southeast, Peter Whipp on *Magic* saw something similar, a halo around a hazy sun with wispy tendrils trailing behind. "I'd read about that," Whipp says. "It said, 'If you ever see that, beware.'"

Alan Jeyes believed there was a chance that the storm would skirt the fleet and move off to the northeast. If that happened, conditions wouldn't be as bad as the forecast. He suggested *Evergreen* would look foolish if they gave up now, an embarrassing conclusion to a miserable series. Jeyes was glued to the radio from then on and heard each of the more frequent and urgent forecasts. At 8:50 p.m., the Met Office called for a full gale for most of Ireland – imminent Force 9. There would be gusts in the fifties. The Beaufort scale description of seas at this wind speed is sobering: "Very high waves. Dense streaks of foam along the direction of the wind. Crests of waves begin to topple, tumble and roll over. Spray may affect visibility."

*Evergreen*'s crew looked to Steve Killing for assurance about the boat; after all, he had helped to build it. Killing was an engineer who worked for C&C Yachts and had overseen the boat's construction. A quiet man, he is calm, unflappable, and has a wry sense of humour. Killing felt on the spot because he considered *Evergreen's* strengths to be his successes, her weaknesses, his failures.

"I didn't really know my forces, but I knew that Force 12 was a hurricane," Killing says. "And we were already getting up to Force 9 and 10. Finally, we looked at one another and said, 'This isn't racing any more.'"

While *Evergreen* was being forced to sail closer to the wind – a noisy and lumpy ride – *Magistri* was able to bear off. The sailing was fast and not too uncomfortable, certainly no worse than a bad day on Lake Michigan. Certainly not as bad as that memorable one on Lake Superior. Chuck Bentley was running the normal watch system of three hours on and four hours off, with everyone who was not working resting safely below.

Although the dean, as Nick DeGrazia was known, had sailed in all the big lake races, he was a novice at ocean racing. As word spread about the severity of the approaching storm, he didn't know what to expect.

"I had experienced thirty knots, maybe thirty-five, but I had never seen anything more than that," he says. "But I had a lot of confidence in the crew and in the boat. We all got harnesses on and kept changing the sails down. It was good sailing at that point. We were flying with the rail down like a bat out of hell."

For all his experience, Bentley didn't know what to expect either. He would occasionally ask Peter Farlinger for his opinion, because Farlinger had weathered two nasty blows in the mid-Atlantic while bringing *Magistri* to Cowes. The team couldn't afford to ship her over, so Farlinger had sailed her to the starting line.

Chuck Bentley (left) uses a tiller extension to steer *Magistri*.
Peter Farlinger is on the right. (*Sharon Green*)

Farlinger had been sailing for only five years and had never even contemplated undertaking such an extended voyage. Then thirty-nine years old, he had just sold his Toronto construction company. After a chance encounter with Chuck Bentley at a regatta, *Magistri*'s skipper invited Farlinger on board, where he passed the unwritten test, eventually becoming one of the boat's owners. He is the sort of man who breaks large problems into its component parts, puts them back together again, and when he's found a solution, he works to achieve it.

Before the transatlantic voyage, Farlinger talked to people who had done it, then reduced the crossing to three steps: leave New York and sail east for at least a day and a half, then head northeast. The first leg would not get him any closer to his destination, but it would put him in the Gulf Stream, which would carry him to

England, missing the fog and sometimes nasty weather off the Grand Banks of Newfoundland.

"The third step is to find the lighthouse and determine whether to go left or right. Once you're away from shore, the number of bad things that can happen are greatly reduced," Farlinger says. "If nothing goes wrong, it's that simple."

Farlinger is still the trim, fit, slightly built man he was then, an introvert who enjoys details and is not easily distracted, who doesn't flap, never shouts, and is not afraid to try new things. All of this stood him in good stead during the twenty-eight-day transatlantic trip, because it wasn't quite as straightforward as he expected. He ran into two storms, neither of them life-threatening, but both damaged the boat. Farlinger says those events were the most depressing part of his Fastnet experience, but that in hindsight they couldn't have happened at a better time, as they exposed weaknesses that later could have been fatal.

The first storm passed without incident, the wind had died and the sun was out, but the sea was still running and *Magistri* was moving awkwardly through the swells. Each time she dropped into a trough and the boat rolled, the mast pressed down and twisted. At one point, Farlinger heard a bang and after a few minutes discovered that a stay on the starboard side had sheared. *Magistri* had three pieces of rod rigging on either side of the mast to support its weight. The bottom and top pieces go straight from mast to deck, while the middle one goes to the end of a spreader, which keeps the rod rigging away from the mast, before it went to the deck. The rod had broken at the end of the spreader, so there was nothing holding up the middle section of the mast. "It was just a matter of time before we lost it," Farlinger says.

The crew forged a repair with spare wire rigging carried for just this possibility, and six hours later *Magistri* was back underway.

Two days later, during the second storm, the stay on the other side broke in exactly the same place. "I was as depressed as I've ever been," Farlinger says.

In Cowes, the temporary repairs were replaced with new rigging. Farlinger speculates that the cause of the failure was that the shrouds were overtightened when the mast was rerigged after his trip through the Erie Canal to New York. "We were just dumb lucky," he says. "In the Fastnet, the mast would have broken, the boat would have rolled again and again and again, and we would have died."

When Bentley asked him what might happen to *Magistri* in the storm they were now amid, Farlinger said he figured it would be similar to what he'd sailed through during the Atlantic crossing: an uncomfortable and wet stretch, lasting twelve to eighteen hours, and then it would be gone. *Magistri* could handle it.

Dennis Hogarth cooked a big pot of spaghetti the easy way, boiling it in sea water, perhaps reasoning that, since the water was already salty, he wouldn't need to add any salt. John Hollidge was the first to taste the meal and was almost instantly sick. Then the pot flew off the stove, which the crew took as a sign. There wasn't going to be any dinner, and, as Andre Calla says, "We knew it was going to be bad."

Around that time, some fifteen miles or so to the east, *Pachena's* crew realized that the hoped-for wind shift that would allow them to come up toward Fastnet was not going to happen. They couldn't keep heading north forever, because they would eventually be driven ashore on the south coast of Ireland. So *Pachena* hardened up and turned more into the wind.

Then the first of the big waves started breaking over *Pachena's* bow. During races, the cockpit crew sit on the high, or windward, side of the boat, facing the ocean. They hang their feet over the side while they hug a lifeline, so their weight will keep the boat flatter, allowing it to move faster. They couldn't do this now because of the sting of the wind and spray. Instead, they faced the cockpit, wrapping their arms around the lifeline, and wedged themselves in place.

Mike Schnetzler remembers the moment they realized just how rough this storm was. A wave that was bigger than the others before it arched over the bow then broke, rushing down the deck like a flash flood in a narrow canyon. He was the first to feel the impact and was swept back along the rail into a winch.

"I thought I had broken my leg," Schnetzler says.

Doug Race was disappointed. For the first time in a few weeks, he had been dry, and now he knew he was going to get wet again. As a foredeck guy, Race's job was to help change sails. All evening, he was up and down the deck, shortening the sail bit by bit. Between 6:00 p.m. and 9:00 p.m., the main was reefed and reefed again and then the smallest head sail was replaced with a storm jib. "It was a real adventure," he says.

Race was among the most experienced sailors on board, a lanky and energetic thirty-four-year-old lawyer. He was another West Coast native who had sailed out of the Royal Vancouver Club, graduating from its sailing school and becoming an instructor. When he got his law degree from the University of British Columbia in 1970, he said, "The hell with it" and went sailing. He bummed around Hawaii, sailed across the Atlantic to England, and in 1971 raced in the Fastnet on an English boat. After that, he decided it was time to grow up, and he came home to practise law. He had been a regular part of *Pachena's* crew since 1972. "It was a great deal," says Race, who today runs a law firm in Squamish, B.C. "John's boats were always competitive, state of the art, with good crews. It was a dream."

His companion on the foredeck was the sure-footed, even-tempered Glenn Shugg. Shugg, twenty-five, had graduated from the B.C. Institute of Technology in the spring of 1976 and had also taken a few months off to go sailing. Shugg was strong, and his forte was sail changes and sail trim, handling the spinnaker poles and sheets. Fifteen months and fifteen thousand sea miles later, Shugg had completed a Victoria-to-Maui race, crewed on an eighty-footer called *Anaconda* in the 1976 Sydney-to-Hobart race in Australia, and had done the 1977 Fastnet on *Ballyhoo*, a seventy-three-footer from Australia.

He had weathered a severe storm before, when he had helped deliver *Ballyhoo* from San Francisco to England for the 1977 Fastnet. They crossed the Pacific to Sydney and then dipped about 150 miles south into the fringe of the Southern Ocean, sailing to Fremantle on Australia's west coast. During that storm it had been dark and grey too, and he had seen fifty knots and thirty-foot waves. Now he hoped that what lay ahead was nothing close to that.

Shugg, Race, and Schnetzler were by now close to the bottom of their bag of tricks and about to change down to the smallest sail they had, next up from a storm jib. The wind was blowing so hard, Schnetzler recalls, it turned the sail cloth into a solid sheet. Trying to grab the cloth with wet hands was like trying to pick up a sheet of steel from the middle rather than the edge. It was almost impossible.

Shugg had a harness on, but there were no jacklines to attach himself to, so he went hand over hand toward the bow. Halfway there, he reached the wire shrouds that ran down each side of the mast to the deck and clipped his harness onto the shroud closest to the bow. The spreader lights were on, casting a thin glow in the driving rain. He took the blue sail bag out from under his arm. The sail had been packed with the ropes, which would be run to either side of the cockpit for trimming the sail. Race would tend to the ropes while Schnetzler helped raise the sail once it was anchored to a hook on the deck, slid into its track, and clipped onto the halyard that raised it. For now, Shugg was hugging the mast, his feet wrapped around it for purchase while he hooked on the halyard. All that remained was to move forward, get the sail in the track, and gesture to Schnetzler to hoist. This meant crab-walking to the bow while dragging the bag and the sail, keeping the ropes untangled, maintaining balance, and trying to see in the blinding spray.

He made it to the bow just as a wave lifted the stern, pushing the boat's nose down, and a second wave, coming from another direction, broke over the boat. Shugg grabbed the bow pulpit with his free hand before he was blown straight back, off his feet. "I was weightless," he says. "The wind was blowing me back like a flag. They say adrenalin makes you strong. I tell you, that hand sure wasn't going to let go."

*Pachena* shook off the waves and rose on another, dropping Shugg back to the deck. He lay there for a moment, then hooked his left arm around the lower rung of the pulpit and used it to reach the horn – a J-shaped hook on the deck – where he attached the ring on the sail's tack, or front corner. He knelt and fed the sail in the track as Schnetzler hoisted. Safely back in the cockpit, he reflected on what had just happened.

"I was thinking to myself that this is the ocean, and the ocean plays for keeps."

John Simonett and Steve Tupper tried to ease the tension among the worried crew by downplaying the severity of the storm and predicting it would quickly blow itself out.

"Steve or I would say, 'Hang in, guys, it isn't going to last much longer,'" Simonett says. "We did that about three times over several hours, and finally somebody said, 'Will you guys shut up. Every time you say something, the wind pipes up even more.' We thought we would get three, maybe four, hours of big blow, it would taper off, but this kept building and building for six to eight hours."

As night fell, Don Martin had a creeping feeling the worst was yet to come. "I believed I was immortal until that night in the Irish Sea," he says. "But I learned I wasn't, and that's a pretty big lesson to learn, particularly when you learn it instantly."

# 7

# *Transition*

**"When you do the common things in life in an
uncommon way, you will command the attention
of the world."**

– GEORGE WASHINGTON CARVER

$T$HE DIFFERENCE between a gale and a survival storm is that in
winds up to about fifty knots, the skipper and crew retain control
of the boat and can take measures to do what they think is best. In
a survival storm, with wind speeds approaching hurricane strength,
the "wind and sea become masters," says Adlard Coles in *Heavy
Weather Sailing*, the offshore racing bible. The crew struggle to stay
alive one minute at a time, hoping conditions will ease enough to
give them back control of the boat. The waves are breaking and
tumbling like surf on a beach, sometimes burying the boat with
tons of water.

The only thing a crew can do is to manoeuvre the boat so that
it moves along the wave crests without being swamped or rolled
over – like a surfer trying to find the pipe. The difference in the
conditions between the upper end of Force 8 and Force 10 is the

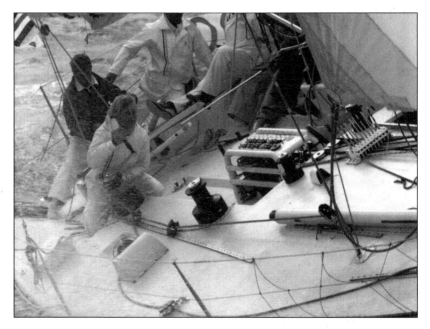

Al Megarry tightens the jib on *Evergreen*, while behind him John Fitzpatrick plays the mainsail. Alan Jeyes is steering. (*Sharon Green*)

difference between the sniffles and pneumonia. The spray is blinding, it is difficult to be heard above the noise of the wind, and every muscle is clenched in the effort to brace against the boat's heel. It takes enormous strength to hold a course, and seasickness may be knocking off the crew one by one.

Between 8:00 p.m. and 10:00 p.m., as the storm arrived in its full fury, most of the fleet was in transition from ocean racing to survival mode. What each crew did or didn't do as the system rolled over them could make the difference between life and death later on. The choices were based on experience, but no amount of experience can overcome bad luck, and some boats simply ran out of luck. But for the most part, the preparations, right or wrong, helped the crews live through something that few experience and fewer still live to talk about.

Don Green's crew was not aware of the fear that gripped his heart. Green felt a huge sense of responsibility, as any skipper does, but more so because he had known that *Evergreen* should not have been in this race. Against his better judgment, he had agreed to go. Now his worse fears had come true. He was sailing what was tantamount to a dinghy into the teeth of a North Atlantic gale.

Around 9:00 p.m., Green decided to withdraw from the race and gathered what crew could be spared and explained his decision. As embarrassing as withdrawal might be, he believed it to be prudent. Ron Barr was at the helm when Green came out of the forward hatch and crab-walked along the deck, one hand clutching the lifeline and the other whatever he could grab, to deliver the news. The motion of the boat was getting awkward and the wind's noise made it difficult to hear what was being said. Green kneeled in front of him and said, "Ron, this is going to get worse and it's coming straight at us. We should get out of here."

"He didn't have any argument from me," Barr says.

*Evergreen* was on the southeast corner of the Labadie Bank, a relatively shallow part of the Western Approaches, though still hundreds of feet deep. They were about 180 miles west of Bristol, the nearest big port. Navigator Jeyes had not brought charts of western England on board, which irritated Green, as entering an unknown port at night, with a following storm surge, is about as dangerous as it gets. Heading north to Ireland was ruled out as the wind could well continue to move through west to northwest, forcing *Evergreen* to beat upwind. So they decided to make a run for Plymouth, 150 miles away. It was a more protected port, and the direction there meant *Evergreen* would take the waves on the stern quarter, a safer and more stable angle to the wind. Their only other options were to heave to or lay ahull. When a boat heaves to, the tiller and storm sail are lashed in opposite directions, the bow stays just off the wind, and the boat drifts slowly downwind. In lying ahull, all sail comes down and the crew goes down below and prays. Green rejected both options in favour of moving, however uncomfortably, toward a port.

Green had already made two important decisions. He left his ego and pride in his pocket by withdrawing before it was too late, then he chose the safest port, though not the closest. The route to Plymouth offered plenty of sea room, kept *Evergreen* away from rocks and shoals, and was in a direction that allowed the most control over the boat.

"Fortunately, we did the right things, and in the end it saved us," he says. "I knew then that it was the beginning of a survival situation. There is nothing worse than a storm in unfamiliar waters in the middle of the night. It's pitch black, confusion can set in, you can become disoriented. I had been through this, and so I knew what was coming."

Don Green's family belonged to the Royal Hamilton Yacht Club, and by the age of twelve, Green was spending his summers racing wooden dinghies called Snipes. As a young teen, he taught sailing at summer camp. But his greatest experience was the eighteen months he spent sailing around the world after he finished high school. It taught him respect for the sea and its many moods and what to expect from a group of people when they encounter weather that has the potential to take their lives. Green was part of a crew put together by Irving Johnson, a noted adventuring sailor. Just after the Second World War, Johnson bought an old steel brigantine, hired as crew young men and women with no experience, and then taught them how to work the ship. They made landfalls in the Galapagos Islands and at Pitcairn Island, home of the *Bounty* mutineers. They visited Borneo, French Indo-China, Bali, Papua New Guinea, the New Hebrides, and Guadalcanal.

For nine days in the Gulf of Siam, the ship endured a typhoon, an experience that taught Green a great deal about heavy-weather sailing. He learned what can happen to people and boats in the teeth of severe storms and how people give out long before boats. He became an expert at trimming sails and steering, learned how to read clouds for weather clues, what different smells on the wind mean, and a great deal about himself. Green applied all that experience to his judgment of this storm and braced himself for the worst.

Al Megarry remembers those transitional hours as the time when he grew up. Megarry was an able sailor, sure and calm and careful in all conditions. He was nineteen, handsome and charming, and like most young men his age, he thought mostly of girls, pubs, and girls. And since his sailing experience had only ever been within sight of shore, he sort of figured ports were always close by. So it was with complete innocence that he asked Dennis Aggus where they were heading as *Evergreen* turned around.

Aggus was a tall, beefy guy with legs like tree stumps and arms like braided steel wire. He was prized because his size and strength came packaged with a good nature, an even temper, and a willing attitude. He was always happy to pitch in whenever and wherever his help was needed.

Then thirty-one, Aggus had already sailed in many of the most challenging Great Lakes races, as well as in some winter regattas in Florida. He had even crewed for one season with Chuck Bentley on the first *Magistri*. For Aggus, sailing was more about the journey than reaching the destination. He cherishes shared experience and common goals. A photograph taken as *Evergreen* crossed the finish line in September 1978 to win the Canada's Cup shows everyone on board with their arms raised in elation, except for Aggus, who is sitting head down, deflated. The journey was over.

But this journey was not unfolding as planned. Aggus answered Megarry's question with one of his own. "I said, 'Al, we're 150 miles away from shore, where do you want to go?'"

Steve Killing was making sure that everything on board was lashed down tightly, that gear was securely stowed, and safety harnesses were on and attached to jacklines. Down below, anything that might become a lethal weapon once airborne – pots, cans of food, utensils – was put away. Dennis Aggus, having learned the lesson during a big blow on Lake Michigan, took all the figure-eight stop knots out of the end of the ropes running into the cockpit. Figure-eight knots are used to prevent lines from running out of their stoppers, should the stoppers accidentally open. The line runs out as far as the knot. But during a severe storm, the wind could run the line out and jam the knot with such force that it would be impossible to haul back in. Then the slack line would let the sail fill like a kite with the potential for a broach or capsize.

Killing felt guilty about quitting, even though he knew it was the right thing to do. "You wonder whether you're being wimpy," he says. "You second-guess yourself, because you don't know whether other people have made the same decisions or are even having any problems."

Before *Evergreen* turned around, the crew's last act was to reduce its mainsail to its smallest size and replace the headsail with the storm jib. The waves were by now ten to twelve feet high and the wind gusting to thirty knots. The boat did not need the storm sail, but by thinking ahead, the crew avoided having to change the sail when it was almost impossibly difficult to do so.

Even so, that last sail change took four crew members. They clipped their harnesses onto the jacklines and inched their way to the bow. Megarry pulled the sail down and unclipped the halyard. Jim Talmage fell on the sail to stop it from blowing overboard.

Killing clipped the halyard onto the storm jib and fed the sail into the track. Megarry tied the lines onto the foot of the sail that led back to the cockpit. In the cockpit, Dennis Aggus used his formidable strength to winch the sail up the track.

It took the better part of a half-hour to complete. It was one hand for the boat and one for the task. They lost their balance, they fell, and they were flung to the end of their lifelines and into the air as the boat drove off the waves. Their muscles ached with tension because there was nowhere to brace themselves. They bounced off stanchions, scraped along the deck, or were thrown against any one of a dozen sharp objects. Finally, they shoved the sail through the hatch, crawled back into the cockpit, and collapsed.

"It was two pulls on the sail and then hang on as you go under," Killing says. "As we got it half down, the wind hits, whammo. All of a sudden it was blowing about forty knots."

It was 9:40 p.m.

Everyone knows that a little stress can be a good thing. It's hard to study if you don't have a test, tough to write up a report unless there's a deadline. We learn better and faster if we're under some pressure. This may explain why many of the sailors would later say the 1979 Fastnet was the most exhilarating and intensely felt event of their lives, even though they found it terrifying.

Fear is accompanied by physiological changes that alter behaviour and help us cope. Our emotions urge us to do things quickly, without thinking. Thinking takes time and in a moment of crisis slows you down. Our immediate physiological response is a jolt of adrenalin, one of several stress hormones that shut down non-emergency functions such as digestion and sex drive and direct the body's resources to fighting or fleeing. As the adrenalin flooded their nervous systems, it brought a heightened sense of awareness, faster reactions and more acute hearing, an ability to think and act more quickly, and split-second responses that were not normally possible. Now they could hear the faintest sound, see the slightest movement. Their hand-eye coordination improved, and their focus narrowed.

Stirling Moss, one of the great racing-car drivers of the 1950s and 1960s, once explained the excitement that fear gave him: "You go around a corner absolutely flat out, right on the ragged edge, but absolutely in control. . . . You stay just on this side of that fraction of extra weight that could ruin everything and perhaps kill you, and you are on top of it all, and the exhilaration, the thrill, is tremendous."

Moss is describing the emotional state where the chemicals are at the optimum mix. Too much of them, you get panic and physical and mental collapse. This is because in addition to turning on the juice, brain chemistry also interferes with memory. This is why most people under stress are incapable of performing any but the simplest of tasks. The world shuts down, focus narrows, context is lost. You see less, hear less, and miss more cues.

As a group, the Admiral's Cup sailors were responding well to the deteriorating conditions. Most of them were elite performers, with experience in high-risk sailing conditions. More than a few were thrill-seekers, those who tackle extreme situations to feel more alive. They can thrive on the stress and harness it, managing their fear in a way other people can't. They don't get rattled. They don't panic. They don't freeze. They would long since have given up ocean racing if they were afraid of wind, waves, and storms. As the sailing got harder, they just buckled down and got on with it.

Peter Cowern, the mild-mannered financial analyst aboard *Magistri*, took up sailing as an adult because he enjoyed the energy of teamwork, the mental arithmetic of navigation, and the exhilaration of racing. Cowern's other hobbies are skydiving and scuba diving. "Do I have a high fear threshold?" he says. "I do, actually. I'm an adventuresome sort."

A New Zealander who came to Canada to attend university, Cowern describes his upbringing as "rough and tumble." He enjoyed contact sports such as judo and rugby. He says he was not afraid at all during the Fastnet race. "I'm not one to get fazed too much, too quickly."

*Pachena's* John Simonett also relaxes by scuba diving. He has a small-plane licence and owns a thirty-six-foot salmon-fishing boat. He is startled when asked if he was afraid during Fastnet.

"I wouldn't characterize what I felt as fear," he says. "It was more a highly developed awareness, if you know what I mean. There was a large element of danger, but it wasn't fear. I felt alert: Don't screw anything up, pay attention, that sort of thing."

Chuck Bentley had much the same reaction. As the storm grew in intensity, demanding more of his attention, his focus narrowed and, like Simonett, he became more aware of the sounds and feel of his boat, felt the power of the waves as he threaded a path through them. On a pitch-black night, in seas that reached the height of a four-storey building, with the wind gusting to hurricane strength in a forty-two-foot fibreglass boat, Bentley was feeling in harmony with the ocean. He maintains that a good helmsman has to feel the sea. And even though he was very tired, he was able to detect patterns in the chaotic winds and waves. Bentley also felt the weight of the crew's confidence and expectations. They had, in effect, elected him to lead them. "If you're the person who everybody looks to, you deal with the conditions and get on with it," he says.

Arch Alyea, who would spend much of that night on *Magistri's* deck, is another man with a high fear threshold. Alyea was born and raised in Belleville, Ontario, and as a teen landed a job at C&C Yacht's first boatyard there. He has hung around boats ever since. Although his first name is Arthur, he's been known as Arch or Archer ever since he sailed with a Dane who couldn't quite get the "th" right. It so amused his sailing buddies that the name stuck. Alyea was another of those who had survived *Magistri's* natural selection. Trained as an engineer, with a degree in geology and an M.B.A., Alyea is technically inclined. He has a slow, deliberate way of speaking, and an observer can almost watch the thoughts form in his head. Alyea doesn't so much enjoy danger as enjoy overcoming it.

"Bentley and I are almost the same," he says. "We go down the same set of tracks."

Alyea takes pleasure in sailing because the sport takes him up against all of nature's whims – the gentle and magical, the harsh and dangerous. He says that the knockdown on Lake Superior that scared Chris Punter to death was "a great ride." Like Peter Cowern and *Evergreen's* Dennis Aggus, Alyea likes the paradoxical simplicity and complexity of handling a boat, and the sense of belonging offered by team effort and shared accomplishment. On board, his world is reduced to doing his task as perfectly as he is able. The big thinking belongs to someone else. As his wife, Lynda, says, "Arthur is totally focused on the moment, which is why he is able to go through these things without breaking."

There were other men such as Arch Alyea at sea that night. The danger was real, but a bit removed, as they moved their boats forward, with the goal of rounding Fastnet Rock, surviving the storm, and finishing the race. In some cases, they were so focused they were surprised at how deadly the conditions actually were and realized only much later how lucky they were to be alive. *Pachena's* Mike Schnetzler says, "There was never a scary moment for me.

This had to be done, that had to be done. You're thinking about the task at hand. But I'm the type of guy who says this is what we have to do and then figures out how to do it."

But other sailors were quite sensibly terrified, in fear for their lives, wondering if they would live to see the pink glow of sunrise. Their task, perhaps more difficult, was to control their fear and not panic. Panic in storm conditions can be fatal because the overwhelming emotional response is to do something, anything, that smothers reason and can lead to the wrong decision. Later that night, many crews unnecessarily abandoned ship, fearing their boat was sinking, and got into rubber life rafts. The rafts were far less seaworthy. Perversely, they feared that their much larger, much better built boats, designed for ocean sailing, were *less safe* then a raft made of vulcanized rubber just a few millimetres thick. In all, twenty-five boats were abandoned and 135 people rescued, many from life rafts. Yet, in all but five cases, their boats were found afloat, more or less intact, certainly in better condition than the life rafts.

Crews that didn't panic were usually the best trained, were well led and had sailed with one another for some time, were disciplined, and trusted their leaders. They had faith in the soundness of their boats, had experienced bad weather before, and although the severity of this one was beyond anything they had known, they continued to function and to do what was necessary, even though they may have been very afraid.

Don Green had weathered a typhoon, and Dennis Aggus and Ron Barr had extensive lake sailing experience, as well as some in the open ocean. Alan Jeyes had sailed in a previous Fastnet. The *Magistri* and *Pachena* crews had been challenged many a time. They knew one another's limits and had faith in themselves and their skipper.

Author Glin Bennett writes, "The greater the mastery, the greater the feeling of being able to do something about one's circumstances."

This may explain experienced sailors' reluctance to heave to, even when their lives are in peril. It is a good tactic for short-handed crews who can become exhausted battling storms. Full crews and racing crews rarely use it because running off, as *Evergreen* did, provides the best antidote for fear: action.

"Thank goodness we anticipated the worst," says Don Green. "The trick is to stop anything from going wrong. Stay on top of it, be prepared, because one thing leads to another."

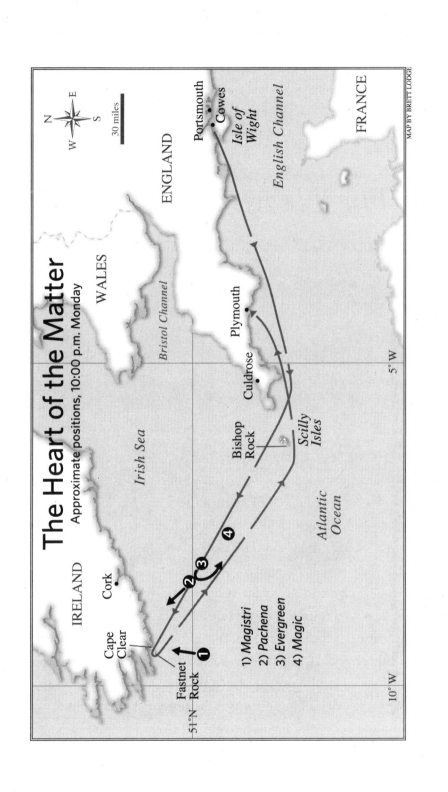

# The Heart of the Matter
Approximate positions, 10:00 p.m. Monday

IRELAND

Cork

Cape
Clear

Fastnet
Rock

51°N

WALES

Irish Sea

Bristol Channel

ENGLAND

Portsmouth
Cowes
Isle of
Wight

English Channel

Plymouth

Culdrose

Bishop
Rock

Scilly
Isles

Atlantic
Ocean

FRANCE

1) *Magistri*
2) *Pachena*
3) *Evergreen*
4) *Magic*

N
W E
S

30 miles

10°W

5°W

MAP BY BRETT LODGE

# 8

# *The Heart of the Matter*

**"Things are never so bad they can't be made worse."**

– HUMPHREY BOGART

$\sim\sim\sim\sim\sim\sim\sim$

$W$HEN *KIALOA*, skippered by Los Angeles real estate executive Jim Kilroy, rounded the Fastnet at about 1:00 p.m. on Monday, August 13, the wind was blowing at between ten to fifteen knots. *Kialoa* was leading the fleet and eight hours later was more than halfway back to the Channel, heading away from the storm. *Condor of Bermuda*, which *Evergreen* would meet later that night, rounded in second place, at 2:00 p.m. At 6:30 p.m., Ted Turner's sixty-one-foot *Tenacious* rounded Fastnet in a gentle swell and light breeze. The Fastnet Rock looked to Turner's son Teddy Jr., "as kind of English pretty." It wasn't long before the winds and waves built, and as *Tenacious* began the 230-mile journey back to Plymouth, what most worried her crew was the potential for a collision with one of the boats heading to the rock. As the storm built throughout the evening, it was clear that any contact, whether a glancing blow or solid strike, would sink both boats, with little chance of rescue.

"That was terrifying," Turner says. "We were used to seeing running lights on deck, and here they were on the masts, but you couldn't see them except at the top of waves. That's how big the waves were, and that was part of the rescue problem. The conditions were so bad that if you saw people in trouble, what could you have done? We would have been hard-pressed to help anyone."

*Tenacious* took in a reef and by midnight had taken in two more and was flying her smallest working jib. She was making ten knots, though later the knotmeter would hit twelve and stay there. On analog instruments, twelve knots was as high as it went. Even racing machines rarely hit those speeds in the late 1970s. They never knew for sure the real strength of the wind, Turner says. Their wind-speed instrument went as high as sixty knots, and once it reached sixty, it stuck there for a while, and then the cups at the top of the mast that measured speed were blown away. The instrument stopped reading altogether.

As *Evergreen* turned back to Plymouth, her last official act of the 1979 Admiral's Cup was to notify the Dutch destroyer *Overijssel*, the guard ship for the race, that she was withdrawing. The transmission was acknowledged but not passed on to race headquarters. By the time *Evergreen* made the call, most of the fleet was in difficulty, and the race committee asked the Admiral's Cup boats to stay off the air. Until then, they had been required to check in at three-hour intervals. Once the fleet stopped checking in, they effectively vanished. Their positions and intentions were unknown, and the next day many anxious friends and relatives assumed they were dead.

Between 10:00 p.m. and midnight, the wind moved rapidly through Force 7, 8, and 9 to 10. The wind direction changed from southwest to west and then northwest. Instead of a long, lazy fetch from one direction, the waves became short and steep and incredibly high, coming from several directions at once, buffeting boats one way and then the other. That was the killer, not the wind. The waves were chaotic, which only aggravated the fear and seasickness, depleting the crews of people to drive the boats at their moment of greatest need.

The size and shape of waves depends on the strength of the wind, how long the wind has blown from a certain direction, how deep the water is, and whether there is current to affect them. On an average twenty-five-knot day in the Southern Ocean, where there is no land to interrupt the motion, waves may be half a mile or more from crest to crest, with a wave height of forty feet. The swells in this aquatic wilderness are often called Ocean Himalayas. Novices are petrified when they look over their shoulders to see what appears to be a green wall about to engulf them. But boats ride up the swell and gently down the other side.

Oceanographers have developed mathematical models that can predict wave height and length, and in his book *Oceanography and Seamanship*, William Van Dorn offers examples. A twenty-knot breeze blowing over one hundred miles of deep ocean for twelve hours makes waves six feet high. Double the wind speed to forty knots over that same one hundred miles of ocean and suddenly the waves aren't six feet but thirty feet.

Many of the Fastnet Admiral's Cup sailors had sailed in the winter SORC series off Florida, where a moderate wind blowing against the current of the Gulf Stream can create frightening waves. Pounding through them hour after hour makes it feel as if the boat is disintegrating. Sleep is impossible because of the noise, and there isn't a comfortable place to rest and relax weary muscles. Fatigue and sleeplessness round out the agony. *Magic* had encountered waves like these during the wind-against-tide night that forced her to put in at Dartmouth.

Depth of water is another influence on wave height. When wind-driven waves encounter shallows, or shoals, their height increases. Once a wave reaches so high that the base can no longer support the top, it starts to tumble and becomes a breaker. A helmsman trying to navigate such seas has the unenviable job of ensuring that the wave doesn't collapse on top of the boat. Van Dorn writes that the impact of a breaker in a survival storm can exceed a force of one ton per square foot, roughly equivalent to dropping an average-sized sailboat into calm water from a height of thirty-two feet. Water squirts through every small crack, pinhole, or hatch, and those on deck have even odds of being swept away. If they have lifelines on, they stay with the boat, unless the webbing or the attachment point snaps. In the best circumstances, the boat shakes off the water and staggers on her way. At worst, the boat goes into a death spiral like a log rolling down a hill.

Every boat has a point beyond which it cannot right itself. When a boat is near that point, two forces are fighting for supremacy: gravity and buoyancy. Gravity is the force acting on the weight of the vessel and all the things in it, and buoyancy is the force of all the air in the boat trying to rise above the surface of the water. On a sailboat moving easily through the water, the two forces are equal and balance each other along the centreline. When a boat gets pushed to her side, the buoyancy increases because more of the boat is under water and wants to pop up. But if pushed over too far, there comes a point when, with the keel out of the water, the deck and cockpit flooded, and the lee rail under water, the boat reaches the "zero-moment," the point of infinite risk. Now, with the vessel spending more time under water, gravity starts to conquer buoyancy. Should anything fail – a hatch bursting open, a window blowing out – gravity wins. As Sebastian Junger says, at that point she's not sailing, but sinking.

That is the danger the fleet faced. The wind was now so strong that the smaller boats could not carry enough sail to steer around waves. Many ceased to move forward at all because they were too small to carry more than storm jibs. John Rousmaniere, who was aboard *Toscana*, calculated that a moderately large breaker that is six feet high and ten feet across moving at thirty knots is a force of twenty-three thousand pounds of moving water. That force is 50. per cent more than *Evergreen* weighed. If you catch a breaker like that at the wrong time, you are right to wonder if this is the end.

By now the spume and foam at the top of waves were being blown sideways. Every fifteen minutes on *Evergreen*, Steve Killing eased or pulled the reefing line that kept the main sail tied down to the boom, so that the lines wouldn't chafe in the same place. The engine was on to keep the batteries charged and to provide manoeuvrability in troughs. Killing was finding it difficult to maintain control of the helm, because whenever *Evergreen* fell off a wave, she would surf down its side and in the lee slow to a halt in the trough. He tried to take each wave on an angle, climbing up the side and pushing the tiller away when the wave began to break so the boat turned into the breaking water and most of it slid under the boat. A misjudgment meant a knockdown, and there were many of both.

"You had a feeling of insignificance," Killing says, "knowing that even though you are ready and hanging on, there's nothing you can do. The wave just flushed you out."

Steve Killing helped design *Evergreen*.
While others worried about the keel,
he was most concerned about the mast.
(*Steve Killing*)

At the height of the storm, *Evergreen* was being knocked down every twenty minutes, and each one triggering the fear that the mast might go, the tiller might snap, the rudder jam, or that the several tons of the boat's retractable keel might punch through the deck, sending the boat to the bottom. It is often a second knockdown coming soon after the first that finishes boats. The vessels are so heavy with water their buoyancy is affected and they're sitting ducks. It was a small mercy – or miracle of design – that *Evergreen*'s much-maligned open transom helped sluice water quickly out the back, allowing the boat to rise quickly and get back on her way.

As day passed into night, *Magistri* altered course toward Fastnet. She was twenty miles farther west than *Pachena* and *Evergreen*, and by about 9:30 p.m., the waves were building. Since nobody had ever seen formations quite like it, the crew came on deck to look, sitting on the windward side, arms locked behind them on the lifelines as they watched the sea roll by.

"It was such an incredible sight," Chuck Bentley says. "We were pretty much awestruck."

Eventually, Bentley realized that if the boat was hit by a breaker, someone could get swept away, so he ordered everyone below except those on watch. By then, the winds were in the high thirties, gusting into the forties. *Magistri* was taking the seas about forty-five degrees off the bow, "a nice diagonal ride," Bentley says. "A wonderful angle of approach, doing eight or nine knots, lifted up and over these seas and down the backside."

John Hollidge, recalling the conditions he'd faced a year ago in the Sea of Japan, was less awestruck. He was thinking about how best to prepare for the worst. "I had seen seas like that, but not the combination we had and the speed with which it came up," he says. "I suppose I'm fatalistic. I tend not to worry, because there's nothing you can do. You just have to prepare for the blow, tucker the boat down, and then sweat it out."

On the foredeck, Fred Goode, Nick DeGrazia, and Chris Punter were sweating even as the temperature fell; the driving rain felt like needles in their eyes. The wind was fitful, gusting and falling back, but getting ever stronger. They had moved steadily through their available sails and were exhausted. The last thing you want to do at night in a storm is change sails, so they kept going down to one smaller than they needed, hoping that would keep them for a while. But the wind was building so rapidly that almost by the time it was set, it was time to change down again. Then, with three reefs in the main, *Magistri* launched over a wave and a gust tore the sail. They dropped the main completely. It was too rough for Andre Calla to effect a repair, but rough enough to go down to the sail of last resort, the storm jib.

Around 11:00 p.m., Nick DeGrazia clipped his safety harness to the toe rail, an aluminum fitting at the edge of the deck with holes in it to attach lines or blocks. He crawled forward, clipping and unclipping his harness as he went. It was so dark he couldn't see what lay ahead unless the boat was riding up the front of a wave and there was a reflection on the surface of the water from the running lights. The waves were twenty feet high, as tall as a double-decker bus, and occasionally the boat flew off the top and landed with a thud.

"I get to the bow, I'm unravelling the sail, and someone yells, 'Hang on!'" DeGrazia says. "So I hang on to the lifeline with one arm and have my other arm wrapped around the sail. My whole body comes off the deck. I'm suspended in water and can feel myself floating. All of a sudden the harness snaps tight, the boat comes out of the wave, and I drop back down on the deck."

DeGrazia had been thrown back eight feet to the length of his tether. Stunned, he lay there for a moment, gasping for breath. Realizing he still had the sail under his arm, DeGrazia crawled back to the bow, hooked his safety line on to the head stay, and slid the storm jib into its slot.

Meanwhile, Peter Farlinger and Chris Punter were crawling forward to help. One eased the storm sail into the slot on the head stay foil while the other helped smother the bigger sail as it was hauled down. Farlinger was not wearing a harness, fearing that the boat was in such peril that he needed to be speedy, not cautious. He timed the boat's lurches with his own movements forward and was fortunate not to be tossed overboard.

"Rightly or wrongly, to me the risk was in taking too long to get the job done," Farlinger says. "You could say I was lucky I wasn't swept off the boat, and it may be true. But, I made a decision that this is something that has to be done *now*, because without the storm jib we couldn't control the boat. We had to get it up to save ourselves."

When Chris Punter had answered the call for all hands, he had grabbed a life jacket. Halfway along the deck he realized he didn't have his harness on and, unlike Farlinger, recalled thinking, This is really stupid.

Farlinger slithered along the deck in a half-crouch, using the lashed-down spinnaker pole as a handhold. When a wave threatened to sweep him away, he was able to wedge his leg under the pole and brace himself. At the bow, he helped get the sail in its slot, made sure the halyard that hauled it aloft wasn't fouled, and moved to the mast where he helped raise it.

The cockpit was the safest place to be, and Peter Cowern was there, firmly clipped on, working the winches to raise the sail. A married man, soon to become a new father, Cowern was comforted by the umbilical cord that tethered him to the ship. It gave him the illusion of safety. Just how illusory became clear some months later when he took the harness to a rigging shop for inspection. They told him the webbing was fine, but the stitching attaching the snap shackle was weak and improperly sewn. They figured it would have broken under the slightest pressure. Sometimes it just comes down to luck.

Arch Alyea was also in the cockpit calmly doing what he had to do. It dawned on him then that *Magistri* had crossed a threshold into an unknown zone. The crew was still in control, but the conditions were beyond anything he had ever known. Reaching at nine knots with a storm jib "that's farther than you've ever been," he says.

Alyea's worry at they headed closer to the Fastnet was the same as Ted Turner Jr.'s. He saw masthead lights blinking in the darkness and assumed they were boats returning to Plymouth. Alyea did some mental arithmetic and figured the impact of two boats would smash both to kindling. He wondered what the odds of a collision were. There were 303 boats on the course, all converging on the same place at more or less the same time. Add zero visibility, twenty- to thirty-foot waves, and a blinding spray, and it came down to more luck. Visibility was so poor that one person peered at the compass, relayed the heading to a second person, who then relayed that to the helmsman. The sensation of the spray, says Alyea, was as if somebody was throwing gravel into your face.

That was about 11:30 p.m. The storm was still several hours from its peak.

Aboard *Pachena*, the crew struggled even harder than the men on *Magistri*, because they were well below the mark and couldn't bear off. Fastnet was fifteen to twenty miles directly upwind. They had to come up and, as much as possible, sail closer to the wind. They were down to their storm jib too. Instead of taking the waves on an angle, they were driving over the top and falling off into the troughs. It was like being the crash-test dummy in a car smashing into a brick wall. By 11:00 p.m., skipper John Newton, who was rarely seasick, was confined to bed. *Pachena*'s navigator pilot, Pat Leslie, was soon to follow. Don Martin would fall later, leaving six people to man the boat through the worst hours of the night. It was fear of becoming sick that kept Mike Schnetzler in the cockpit. Down below, the nauseating motion meant that getting in and out of foul-weather gear was a bruising experience. As you hopped on one foot getting out of the gear, the boat would lurch, bouncing you off the cabin walls and your colleagues.

"I figured what's the point of going below," Schnetzler says. "I was already wet."

Don Martin had sailed through storms before and, like Arch Alyea, his realization of how much danger they were in came only gradually. Until the point when he was felled by seasickness, Martin believed a successful race was a matter of figuring out the tactics that local sailors used to win. "We were still thinking we were rookies and had better keep trying to figure it," Martin says. "We were still trying to win."

With just the storm jib, the boat was horribly unbalanced. Instead of going in a straight line, *Pachena* wobbled back and forth as she moved through the gigantic waves, which John Simonett says were quite impressive. "Twenty-five, thirty feet, occasionally fifty. When it gets fifty feet high, you just wrap your arm around something and hang on. It has to break and it falls straight into the boat. If you are not hanging on, you are gone."

Steve Tupper's frustration was seeing the Fastnet light appear at the top of the waves only to disappear as the boat fell into a trough. It never seemed to get any closer. At about midnight, the wind switched to northwest, pushing *Pachena* toward the Irish coast. Occasionally, he could even see shore lights. Tupper thought that was too close for comfort. If the wind continued to shift, *Pachena* could be driven too far inshore and be shipwrecked. He threw the helm over, and for the next four hours, *Pachena* tacked back and forth, heading due south and then north again, trying to inch closer to Fastnet.

"It didn't seem to matter what we did," Tupper says. "We could see the lighthouse, but couldn't get any closer."

As midnight approached, it took two people to steer *Evergreen*, both gripping the long aluminum tiller to keep her on course. The deck flexed and heaved from the pressure, and as *Evergreen* was swept up by each wave, water broke over one side and raced down her flat deck. Down below, they were manning the bilge pumps. Don Green says it was like Niagara Falls, with water pouring in through the hatches, leaking through the chain plate, and every other place it could. Dennis Aggus cheerfully recalls that the water never got more than ankle deep, just as long as someone was pumping.

Aggus had a towel around his neck to stop the drips from running down his neck, an old racing trick. He wore rubberized gloves to protect his hands and provide grip. As two men steered, Aggus played the mainsail, letting it out at the top of the waves to ease the impact when the wind's full force punched the boat. He had to be careful not to wrap the rope around his hand, as the pressure could have broken every finger had the rope slipped. The friction would have shredded his glove and sliced through the meat of his hand. Easing the sail at the crest of each wave allowed the skipper to pull the tiller toward them to bear off. This kept the boat on a straighter course and overcame *Evergreen*'s tendency to round up into the wind. In the troughs, Aggus muscled the sail back in, so there was enough power to drive up the next wave. At the top, he started all over again.

*Evergreen*'s life raft was in a small compartment underneath the cockpit floor. In his wildest dreams, Steve Killing had never thought he would ever use it, because it implied your ship was sinking or was about to. Just looking at the thing opened up any number of black thoughts, but Killing figured if there was ever a night, it was this one. So he pulled out the canister, dragged it to the base of the mast, and lashed it down.

"I figured if something major happens and we're trying to get the lid off this thing, we're probably under water and never going to make it. So now was the time," he says. All the while, he told the crew not to worry, it was just a precaution, but he remembers the odd look on their faces. Jim Talmage was, if anything, more alarmed by Killing's soothing words. "That's when I said to myself, Holy shit, what's going on here?" Talmage says.

All the while, Ron Barr was steering on the edge, roaring down the waves trying to find the sweet spot between them, missing the curl of the first one and trying to climb up the back of the second. At the top of one wave, Barr spotted a red flare arching through the dark. It was a distress signal. He yelled at Green and altered course.

# 9

# *Monday Midnight*

**"Life is pleasant. Death is peaceful.
It's the transition that's troublesome."**

– ISAAC ASIMOV

ALTHOUGH *MAGISTRI* was less than six hours into the hard sailing, the crew was already at the other side of the earlier adrenalin surge and was growing fatigued. They had been unable to eat or drink, to replenish their energy, so they gradually crashed. Nick DeGrazia lay on the floor of the cabin, willing his muscles to respond to the command of his brain. He was trying to answer a call for help from on deck but could not. "I remember saying, 'I'll go,' and yet I couldn't make my body move," DeGrazia says. "I was saying to myself, You have to get up, you have to get up, and my body was saying, No, we're not moving."

The storm was straining everyone's nervous systems – the jarring motion, the noise, the boat's pitch and toss. They were wet, chilled, and in some cases becoming hypothermic as the temperature dropped to about ten degrees Celsius. The waves hitting the boat and breaking over the deck made one kind of noise. The wind made another, truly intimidating sound, as it squealed in the rigging. They had to shout directly into one another's ears to be heard. Yet they had to listen to the sounds, because it was important to hear any changes. Was it blowing harder or had it eased? Was the roar of the waves indicating that a rogue was coming? Did the sickening thud as the hull landed in a trough mean something had broken? The sounds were cacophonous and hard to decipher because they hadn't been heard before, yet they were vital clues to the health of their small floating world.

After a spell on deck, Andre Calla collapsed below on a pile of wet sails at the bottom of the companionway. Calla, twenty-seven, was a student at University of Toronto's School of Architecture and his job was to trim the jib, the huge sail at the front of the boat. The son of Italian immigrants, Calla had learned to sail on Toronto's waterfront, and at one point drove the tender that ferried members of the RCYC to their island clubhouse.

Peter Farlinger says, "Andre was the prototypical Italian forever-bachelor who may or may not still live with his mother and spend his days doing what young men are supposed to be doing: drinking espresso, going to cafés, dating pretty women.

"Instead of retiring when you're sixty to do all the things you want to do, you do them between twenty and fifty. Most of us have it backwards. Work hard when we're young and plan to play hard afterwards, but we're too old. Andre has always been able to be the guy who mysteriously just flows through life."

On *Magistri*, he was valued for stamina, his great enthusiasm, and his willingness to pitch in whenever and wherever. His job during the race was to tighten or loosen the lines on either side of the cockpit that brought in the sail. They were wrapped around massive winches. It was exhausting, and now Calla lay there, his eyes watering, his beard and thick mane of brown hair matted. He thought that lying on the floor, inches away from oily bilge water, was marginally better than being in a berth. In the berth, just a half an inch or so of fibreglass separated him from tons of green water, and the flexing of the deck and bulkheads was more noticeable.

The floor was on the centreline and so slightly less heeled over. Its coffinlike shape meant you could wedge one way or the other. "I was so tired that taking off my clothes and changing wasted valuable sleeping time," Calla says.

Only the very exhausted or the very lucky got any real rest. Most of the crew was driven to the edge of sanity listening intently, trying to figure out whether the next sound was the death blow. They likened the din to being inside a garbage can that was being kicked down a street, or in an oil drum being beaten by a hammer. Water hissed by the hull, the fibreglass hummed and vibrated, and they were sometimes airborne, enduring fearful seconds before the boat came down again. Some of the crew thought the best place to be was to be wedged in a pipe berth on the windward side of the boat. There at least you could adjust the angle and stay more or less flat. When they had to relieve themselves, they did so in their pants, something they tried to do only while on deck, where it was rinsed away by the storm. Dennis Aggus, *Evergreen*'s cook, felt the affront of the mess down below most keenly. "It was fetid. Fuel, food, sweat. Just dank," he said.

This was why Doug Race and Stewart Jones, like Mike Schnetzler, had no interest in being below as *Pachena* pounded upwind. With three crew seasick, the deck was preferable. Stewart Jones remembers Don Martin coming on deck at one point, convinced *Pachena* was breaking up. Martin had been lying below in darkness and, deprived of all senses except his hearing, had concluded the noises were a death rattle.

"It is always worse down below," Jones says. "It creaks and groans and bangs. You're sick, and your mind goes crazy. It's better to be up there watching the end come."

All through the fleet, there were now continual worries about gear failure, not just pulleys and blocks exploding under pressure, or torn sails and frayed lines. Mechanical systems are in constant motion on a boat at sea, twisting and bending, putting load on their fastenings and fittings. Who really knows when a thing will break, until it breaks. Rather, it was the big stuff that worried them most: structural failures of the masts, rudders, or rigging that could cascade into disaster. *Pachena* had broken her mast once and her crew wondered whether the replacement "telephone pole," as Doug Race called it, would hold. On *Magistri*, two shrouds had snapped on the Atlantic crossing and been repaired in Cowes. Would more fail? Aboard *Evergreen*, thoughts turned to the keel, hammered together in a shed and held on by spot welds. Knowing that, the mast looked all the more fragile.

The crews on deck could see their masts swaying. As long as these aluminum tubes bent forward and backward, or side to side, it was fine. But if the rig was moving forward or backward and also twisting, it was a sign that a dismasting wasn't far away. Take a handful of uncooked spaghetti and give it a twist. It's a pretty good approximation of what can happen.

Masts are fixed to boat by stays, which are made of wire or rod rigging that runs from the mast to attachments on the deck. *Magistri* had three stays on each side of the mast, plus one at the front and two at the back, for nine all told. The two at the back were called running backstays. They are adjustable pieces of rigging that came from the top of the mast to each corner of the stern. When the boat tacked, the running backstay on the windward side was tightened and the one on the leeward side loosened, providing additional

A year earlier, Lt. John Hollidge (shown here) had weathered a typhoon in the Sea of Japan.
(*Arch Alyea*)

support. Chuck Bentley didn't think that arrangement was strong enough, so he took a spare halyard from the mast and led it to the toe rail at the stern, clipped it on and tightened it to buttress the windward side of the mast.

While the rest of the crew thought that they were barely in control, Lieutenant Hollidge was still at his navigation station plotting and figuring. He was a professional sailor, and was as comfortable as one can be in dealing with the hazards of ocean sailing. His nonchalance was calming.

The previous year, he'd survived a white-knuckle episode in the middle of a typhoon. His ship had been so low on fuel that it had little choice but to pull alongside a tanker and stay close enough in sixty-foot waves to refuel. It took close to two hours of trying to manoeuvre the boats into position, and in the middle of the transfer, a rogue wave sent the ship and tanker in separate directions, ripping the refuelling rig apart. They kept at it, spending another few hours putting all the pieces back together, before they eventually succeeded. Hollidge viewed this storm as a similar challenge. You just had to get on with it. They were in a tough situation but managing. "The guys were good sailors, exceptionally good," Hollidge says. "They were just in conditions they hadn't seen before."

He, too, was wondering about the mast and had already worked out in his mind what he would do if it broke; how he would use the spinnaker pole as a jury-rig. He had been aboard a thirty-six-foot sailboat in a race in the English Channel when the boat lost its rudder about twenty miles from the Isle of Wight. The crew tied two spinnaker poles to the stern, streamed them off the transom, and used a system of ropes and pulleys to change the angle of the poles to manoeuvre the boat. Hollidge doubted that it would work for *Magistri*. The conditions were too extreme.

"If we had lost the rudder at that stage, we would have been in serious trouble," he says. "We would have been rolled, without any shadow of a doubt."

On board *Pachena*, Doug Race was making the same calculation about what he would do if something failed. He pondered the many possibilities; a shroud snapping, the mast failing, a broken rudder. He also believed the seas were too violent to use a spinnaker pole with a floorboard should the rudder break. Even so, "My mind was thinking, Where is that pole? Where is the floorboard, how do you hook it on? How would we keep the boat stern on to the wind? You didn't want it broadside, so you wanted to drag something behind you, maybe a sail, or warps. That's what you do in a race, always think ahead. Anticipation is 90 per cent of it."

On *Evergreen*, the crew was also thinking about the possibility that their craft would go down. As the clock inched toward midnight, she had made about fifteen miles to the southeast in the two and a half hours since she had turned around. That put her average speed under storm jib at about six knots. The waves were getting closer together, becoming steeper, and continually breaking, leaving trails of white foam on the water. The boat's low freeboard and flat cockpit offered no protection from the storm, and exhaustion was setting in. At the helm, Ron Barr was imagining that the breakers looked like ice floes and the blown foam was snow. He was wet, for about three days, had slept only irregularly, and hadn't eaten much in twelve hours. Now he was starting to hallucinate. "I saw floating sheets of ice, but I knew they weren't there," he says.

Many sailors hallucinate, often at night when the waves take on strange shapes. Hallucinations are a function of fatigue, and solo sailors are the most susceptible to fatigue, because they are often sleep deprived for long periods of time. Some report hearing voices in the cockpit when they are down below, others see shapes at the bow or passing boats that aren't there. Psychologist Glin Bennett, who has studied the psychological aspects of single-handing, wrote that half of the fleet in the 1972 Observer Single-handed Trans-Atlantic race reported one or more illusions or hallucinations. In the 1890s, during the first months of his circumnavigation in the *Spray*, Joshua Slocum held conversations with the Spanish pilot of the caravel *Pinta*, which was part of Christopher Columbus's fleet. At one point, Slocum became so ill from a combination of seasickness and food poisoning he was delirious and awoke to find a strange man at the helm of his boat. The man looked like a pirate to Slocum, but introduced himself as the *Pinta*'s pilot. He ordered Slocum back to bed and took charge of the *Spray*. Slocum did as he was told and when he awoke some hours later, he found his thirty-foot boat on course and sailing through the storm.

In March 1969, the great solo circumnavigator Bernard Moitessier heard a voice calling him to the front of *Joshua* as he rounded Cape Horn in a gale. The conditions were cruel – storm-force winds and a steep, short, breaking sea. Moitessier was soaked, half-frozen, and hadn't eaten much in two days. He left the cockpit and moved forward to the mast, where, without a tether, he stood for some time as *Joshua* surged through the swells. A voice urged him to keep going, but he resisted, thinking in one part of his mind it was madness to continue. He eventually inched his way back to the cockpit, reduced sail, and went below to warm up.

During his first solo circumnavigation in 1998–99, American racing sailor Brad Van Liew confessed to coming out on deck a number of times to find sails set differently and having no recollection of doing it. At other times he heard noises and thought that the boat was talking to him. In an exhausted half-sleep at one point, he screamed at a non-existent crew to reef sails because it was *their* turn and he was too tired. He says these hallucinations were more frequent when he was new to the sport. With experience, they diminished.

Luckily, Ron Barr was able to talk about his hallucination to Al Megarry, who was helping him steer. This may have kept him from doing something dangerous and perhaps being overwhelmed by the fantasy. Barr's more grounded worry was that the keel would be lethal should the boat be knocked over on its side past horizontal. As *Evergreen* was being laid on her side every twenty minutes or so, this was a distinct possibility.

"When they built the boat, nobody thought it might end up upside down," Barr says. "So now we're wondering if we get rolled, will the keel tear the deck out of the boat."

Steve Killing kept a careful eye on the hydraulic pressure in the running backstays and made a general inspection of the yacht every so often to ensure nothing was chafing or wearing. He wasn't worried about the keel because after the accident in the Solent, the keel barely moved. In the unlikely event *Evergreen* rolled over, Killing believed, the keel would not be able to slide out. He was more worried about the mast. But in his role as chief morale officer, he assured the crew that if the mast were going to break, it already would have done so during the first furious hour of the storm.

Don Green worried about it all: the mast, the rudder, the keel, the crew, morale, and whether this was the last night of his life. His crew did not sense his fear. They saw someone who was confident and in control.

The waves were continually breaking over the boat and threatened to sweep the helmsmen away. Even though *Evergreen* was taking waves on the quarter, between amidships and the stern, some waves were moving faster than the boat. *Evergreen* with her tiny sail was "riding them like a surfboard," Green says. "How big were these waves? As high as sixty feet."

Green looked around at the crew and wondered how close they were to breaking, how near to panic. This was so far beyond the realm of their experience. Green tried to be upbeat, talking to them about home and what everyone was going to do when they got ashore. A lot of the time he was just there and didn't say anything at all.

"The mind works in very strange ways," Green says. "Every sixty seconds a wave is breaking over the boat. You say to yourself that's the wave that's going to do us in. You wait another sixty seconds and another wave comes. Then another sixty seconds, another wave comes. How much of that can you take before your mind starts to drift off into strange areas?"

Green admits that as much as he was afraid, he was exhilarated. "It was the thrill of a lifetime, absolutely terrifying," he says of the paradox. "We were flying and then we'd fall so hard you thought the boat was going to explode, coming down with such a crash that many times we thought it was broken." They may have been on the edge of a disaster, but *Evergreen* was a thoroughbred and, as she galloped over the thundering surf, the crew could feel the power of this glorious manmade machine.


Aboard *Magic*, the crew was now in a race for survival. Just before midnight she lay wallowing in enormous seas, the likes of which none aboard had ever seen, unable to be steered. Her rudder, which had been carefully repaired before the race, was gone, ripped out of the hands of the helmsman and swept into the sea. Had he held on, he would have followed the assembly into the ocean and drowned.

*Magic* was being hurled down the waves, landing like a sack of flour tossed from the roof of a house. At one point as she hit the ocean, Peter Whipp heard a crack. A wooden rib that stiffened the hull had given way. He wondered if this was how it would end – one rib failing, then another, until the boat was critically weakened and broke apart. The wind was moaning as it passed through the metal rigging; the hull was shuddering. The sounds were utterly terrifying. One of the crew was so afraid he was crying and another was intermittently vomiting. Whipp tried to ignore the sounds. "Out of necessity, I just turned them off," Whipp says. "They were safe in their bunks and the three of us had to get on with doing what had to be done." Tim Allison was steering and Whipp and Peter Hoosen-Owen were below, trying to find a weather bulletin on the radio that would explain why the world had gone mad.

When *Magic* climbed to the top of yet another large wave, the tiller was torn from Allison's grip. The force of the water had snapped the bolts that fasten the rudder to the boat like stale bread-sticks and all the equipment was swept away. The boat now had six half-inch holes in her stern where the bolts had been. She could no longer be steered.

The three men were astonished and realized they were that much closer to dying. But they were a tough bunch and did not give in to panic. As conditions deteriorated, they had been prudent, reducing the amount of sail to keep the boat upright and the motion comfortable. All three were in their thirties and had sailed together for years. In the summer, they usually raced in waters not that far from where they were now, cruising the coves and inlets of Britain and Ireland. They knew one another's capabilities and trusted the soundness of the boat.

At first they thought they had just hit a bad patch and that once conditions eased, they would jury-rig a rudder from bits and pieces on board – a spinnaker pole and hatch cover maybe, a sort of Viking steering oar – and head for shore. So they took down all sail and let the rudderless boat drift while Whipp tried to raise the race committee boat by radio. He managed to make contact, but wasn't sure whether the message was understood. Allison set off flares to attract the attention of any nearby boats. They wanted somebody to know where they were, but had no intention of abandoning ship. The vessel was not in danger of sinking and sticking it out was also a matter of pride. They knew they were in peril, but one of the strong attractions of ocean racing is self-sufficiency. When things go wrong, you work your way out of them. You don't just pack up your marbles, call for help, and go home.

Whipp went below to call the race committee on VHF radio, while Allison and Hoosen-Owen got every spare piece of rope they could find. They intended to trail it over the stern, a traditional method of stabilizing a boat in severe weather, because the rope pulls the stern in a straight line with the waves, an easier point of sail.

"It was classic Adlard Coles, and it didn't work," says Hoosen-Owen, referring to the advice offered in the heavy-weather sailing bible. They had also realized that the trailing rope would be a hazard to any boat coming to their aid. It could end up wrapped around a propeller, disabling the approaching vessel. They pulled the rope in, easing the boat's motion. Exhausted, the three men tried to decide what to do next. Then they saw *Evergreen*.

As *Evergreen* neared *Magic*, Steve Killing struggled to the front of the boat, took the tiny storm jib down, and, with the mainsail reduced to its smallest size and the engine on, pulled closer to the drifting *Magic*.

A second flare helped Barr draw a bead, and soon they were near enough to see *Magic*. In the darkness, he heard one of *Evergreen*'s crew ask, "What the hell can we do for them?" Another replied, "We have to help."

Green and his crew didn't know quite what to do. *Evergreen* made wide passes around *Magic*, riding up the waves and falling off into troughs where the boats lost sight of each other. They shouted across the storm but couldn't make themselves heard. If the boats came too close, they could pulverize each other. If *Magic*'s crew wanted to abandon ship, *Evergreen* wasn't sure how it would pick the men up.

The initial plan was to come as close as possible to *Magic*'s stern and heave a life jacket tied to the end of two hundred-foot lengths of rope into the water. In successive passes with the rope trailing in the water, Whipp and his crew would jump in one by one, grab the life vest, and be hauled in. That was what Alan Jeyes and Peter Whipp initially discussed on the radio, and that was what *Evergreen* first tried to do.

Since the attempt would require so much concentration, it was divided into small tasks. It fell to Dennis Aggus to operate *Evergreen*'s engine. He lay face down in the cockpit, his feet hooked around the aluminum frame that guarded the hydraulics. His lifeline was on, for if a breaker swamped the boat he would easily be washed away. Don Green straddled him, yelling for more or less throttle as they closed in on *Magic*. A wave broke over the bow and raced down the deck, burying Aggus and driving ice-cold water up his foul-weather jacket, down his pants, and filling his boots. He felt as if he'd stuck a finger into an electrical socket. Someone else was primed to toss the line.

Everything on *Magic* seemed calm and shipshape to Steve Killing, who could see the three men in the cockpit looking out at them. To Barr, the situation was desperate. "I saw a plywood boat that was getting the shit kicked out of it. The sails were down, the rudder was gone. They were at the mercy of the sea."

Jim Talmage wondered if that might be *Evergreen* in another hour or so. "They were worse off than us, but I don't remember thinking we were lucky," he says.

It took twenty minutes to make one pass and after that the plan changed. It was like being on a teeter-totter. Asking someone to jump into the water was an invitation to certain death. As Jim Talmage says, "I don't think anybody would have lived through that. They were smart to stay where they were."

Killing, Green, and Fitzpatrick discussed options. Clearly, they couldn't get alongside without risking damage. They thought about putting *Magic* under tow, but in those waves, *Evergreen*'s engine produced very little thrust. Both boats would be at the mercy of the storm. Launching a life raft would be just as risky. Thoughts of rescue went out the window. There was no way they could get someone on board.

While *Evergreen* circled, Whipp talked through the rescue options with Alan Jeyes. Everyone reluctantly concluded that, as much as *Magic* was in peril, she was not in imminent danger of sinking. Getting off the boat would be more dangerous than remaining on board.

"It was a comfort to have *Evergreen* there, to see that someone had responded," says Hoosen-Owen. "It made us feel better, but they could really only do one thing and that was get themselves out of there."

Jeyes agreed to relay *Magic*'s location to the race committee, then, with shouts of encouragement from the crew, *Evergreen* resumed course and was quickly lost to the storm.

Peter Whipp considered his options. He ruled out a jury-rigged rudder. As Hoosen-Owen says, "Anything you put into the sea would have been ripped out of your hands. There were waves breaking over the back, waves breaking over the sides, and waves breaking over the front. That's why we battened down."

*Magic*'s auxiliary engine was impossible to manhandle out of the cabin, up the companionway steps, and into the cockpit. The men needed both hands just to hang on. Even if they could have bolted the engine onto its bracket on the stern, it would not have been able to manoeuvre the boat.

Whipp was thankful that earlier in the day he had the foresight to lash everything down and charge the batteries. As much as it could be without a rudder, *Magic* was shipshape. The three men closed the hatch and listened to their seasick and frightened friends as they wondered what the rest of the night held.

"All we could do was sit there," Whipp says.

What Whipp didn't know was that *Evergreen's* message, relayed via *Condor* to shore, was the initial alarm that mobilized a massive air and sea rescue for the race. For the next eighty-four hours, eight helicopters, six naval vessels, and dozens of commercial ships ranged over ten thousand square miles of ocean to rescue the fleet.

# *IO*

# *Another Part of Hell*

**"The best way out is always through."**

– ROBERT FROST

*His* BACK TO the wind, Nick DeGrazia wedged himself in *Magistri*'s cockpit to stop himself from sliding. The distressing answer to his earlier question, How bad can it get? was now clear. It was, lamentably, much, much worse. He had raced in squalls of thirty-five knots on the Great Lakes, but there winds like that don't last long, certainly not long enough to create waves like this: thirty, forty feet high, with the spray flying even higher. He could see the spume illuminated by the masthead light. Out of the corner of his eye, he could also see the wind speed indicator attached to the bulkhead just forward of the hatch leading down to the cabin. For as long as he stared at the instrument, the needle was stuck on the far side, a reading of sixty knots. He bent over and tapped the glass, but the needle stayed put. Must be broken, he thought. This put the wind speed at Beaufort Force 11, just shy of a hurricane. The sea was now covered in long white patches of foam, and everywhere the edges of the waves were blown into froth, pretty much as Admiral Sir Francis Beaufort predicted when he created the Beaufort scale in 1805. To DeGrazia, it seemed as if the needle was trying to bend past sixty. *Magistri* dove off a wave and for the briefest moment in its lee, the needle flickered and dropped back. He was startled: "That's when I realized it wasn't broken, and that it was blowing more than sixty," he says.

On *Pachena*, Steve Tupper was trying to claw closer to Fastnet Rock. Stewart Jones huddled in the cockpit and watched nervously as breakers ripped the wheel from Tupper's hand time and again. The waves hitting the rudder were so powerful that Tupper couldn't hold on and the wheel spun wildly, stopping when the rudder was pushed as far over as it could go. Jones hoped it wouldn't jam, because then they would be truly helpless.

A few hours earlier, this is exactly what had happened to a thirty-seven-footer called *Trophy*, sailing not far from *Pachena*. *Trophy* was owned by Alan Bartlett, a London pub owner with more than twenty years' sailing experience, plenty of it on the ocean, including an earlier Fastnet. At 11:00 p.m., *Trophy* was reaching toward Fastnet at about ten knots with just a small jib when she spotted a flare. Bartlett took a compass bearing on the spot the flare came from, turned on his engine, and shouted below for someone to note the time and position in the ship's log. He planned to ask officials when the race was over to deduct the time spent going to the aid of the distressed boat from his total. *Trophy* had a big diesel engine, but despite its power, it took an hour for her to reach *Allemander*, the distressed boat. They managed to shout across the storm, and *Allemander* said it was fine and did not want to abandon ship.

*Morningtown*, a thirty-nine-foot cruising boat on loan to the race committee as an escort boat, was also standing by. *Morningtown's* job was to monitor radio channels, and it was this vessel some hours earlier that had politely told *Evergreen* to get off the air and stop asking for weather information. The *Morningtown* crew was finding it hard to stay on station, and seeing *Trophy* there, and spotting another flare in the distance, moved away. Soon afterwards, her rudder cable slipped off the steering quadrant. As the crew tried to fix it, somebody on deck saw a dismasted yacht drift by, with a life raft floating not far behind. They realized in horror that the disabled vessel was *Trophy*.

*Trophy* had run into terribly bad luck. Climbing a breaking wave, she had been overwhelmed and pushed back down the wave. The wheel was torn from her skipper's hand and spun with such force that the rudder jammed underneath the boat, exactly as Stewart Jones feared might happen to *Pachena*. No amount of effort could loosen it. There was nothing to be done except ride the storm out, so all the crew, except three, went below. The hatch boards were put into the slots, but a small gap was left to let in fresh air. Not long afterwards, a wave that crewman Russell Smith said was as high as *Trophy's* fifty-foot mast, lifted the boat, tossed her on her side, and then rolled her right over, smashing her mast to pieces. When the boat righted, the mast and its shrouds were wrapped around the bow, there was two feet of water in the cabin, and the engine was dead. Without the mast to counterbalance the keel, the boat swung wildly. During the rollover, skipper Alan Bartlett had gone overboard and was now trapped in a tangle of lines and rigging. Smith had been in the cockpit when the wave struck. As the boat rolled, he was in the water underneath it. The boat kept going through 360 degrees and rolled back up, and Smith found himself back in the boat. It took the astonished Smith and another crewman ten minutes to get Bartlett untangled and back on board. Meanwhile, two others in a panic and without consulting the others decided to abandon ship. They inflated the life raft and tethered it to the side of the ship.

The choice now was either to cut the raft loose and stay with the boat or to abandon the boat, which, though waterlogged, was still afloat. The raft was acting like a sail, dragging the boat along, with its rail in the water, and threatening to drag her under.

Believing another rollover was likely, and that *Morningtown* was nearby, the eight men bet on the small rubber raft. They got in and drifted down to the *Morningtown*, only to learn that her steering was disabled. They shouted across the storm that they intended to stay in the raft, believing *Morningtown* would call in their position for rescue. Before *Morningtown* was out of sight, the raft started to roll. With at least fifteen hundred pounds of body weight in uncontrolled motion, the raft kept on rolling. The crew couldn't find handholds, and they were flung against one another with considerable force. The fifth time the raft rolled over, it split apart, separating into upper and lower rings. Three men were carried away from the rings and only one managed to swim back to the raft. The other two were lost to the storm. "We saw them disappear on the top of a wave," Smith later told *Newsweek.*

That left six men on the two separated rings. They could still see the *Morningtown*'s running lights, but there was no way they could get to her. All through the night they drifted. Then, at about 5:30 a.m., an RAF Nimrod spotted them and dropped a flare. Soon afterwards, the Dutch destroyer *Overijssel* rescued them, but not before a third crewman died of exposure and exhaustion.

"He literally just gave up," Smith said. All because the skipper couldn't hang on to the wheel, the wheel spun too hard, and then jammed against the hull – a small accident that led to catastrophe.

*Pachena* was fifteen miles upwind of *Trophy*, and as the wind shifted to a little north of west the seas became more violent. Near the Irish coast, the change in ocean depth was adding to the height of the waves. The boat was in one piece, the mast was fine, the rudder was fine, everything was working, except, like *Magistri* and *Evergreen*, *Pachena* didn't have a storm trysail and so couldn't go upwind.

"We were slamming into the seas and falling off," Doug Race says. "It felt like an elevator. You would lift off the seat and then bang, you slammed down. It was a strong aluminum boat, so we didn't worry that it would fall apart. But you always think about losing the mast."

Knockdowns and broaches were frequent now, and among the wind and waves was an uncanny phosphorescence. Whenever water washed over the boat, the deck glowed for a moment or two. The crew had seen this phenomenon before on wild nights in the Pacific Northwest, but in the heart of the Irish Sea in this monstrous storm, it was as chilling as it was spectacular. Steve Tupper tightened his grip on *Pachena*'s wheel and braced himself as the boat rose to take the next wave. The wind was blowing so hard the droplets that splattered his glasses streamed to the side of the lenses. It improved his vision, not that there was much to see. Tupper was looking for different shades of grey, just enough contrast to discern the jagged edge of blown foam at the top of the breaker, allowing him to estimate height, distance, and time to impact.

The former coach of Canada's Olympic sailing team had been playing this game for hours now. He estimated this one to be fifty feet high from bottom to top, as tall as a five-storey house, no worse than others he had been steering around for hours, not even as big as some he'd seen once in a Mediterranean *mistral*. He leaned, squinting into the wind, one broad hand gripping the lifeline and the other on the wheel. Where was the edge? Tupper heard rather than saw the wave approach and instinctively turned the boat away from the oncoming water. He was trying to gather speed so he could turn back and climb up the inside before it curled and broke. He knew right away it wasn't going to work. The boat felt sluggish and unresponsive.

Moments earlier, Simonett had moved to the low side of the boat, perhaps to tighten a line or a jib sheet, he doesn't remember. His harness was clipped on to a stanchion base, but he wasn't holding on to anything, and he didn't see the wave. It swept down the deck and Simonett was thrown overboard, jerking to a stop when he reached the end of his tether.

Jones watched his friend go over, fear constricting his chest and adrenalin flooding his nervous system. He leaned over the side, grabbed Simonett's tether, and hauled him back into the boat. Jones was five-foot, ten-inches tall and weighed one hundred and sixty pounds. Simonett was six inches taller and forty pounds heavier.

"Stew couldn't have done that normally on a bet," Simonett says. "All of a sudden I was flying back onto the high side of the boat." Glenn Shugg, watching from his perch on the rail, marvelled at Jones's newfound strength. "It was just a thing of beauty," he says.

There was barely time for Tupper to be angry at his own miscalculation before he felt the blow, a giant fist being driven deeply into his guts. Gasping, he staggered back into the stainless-steel rail, the impact bending him double. As tons of water roared over the boat, Tupper was swept out the stern, hanging half in and half out as the boat was flicked on her side, the mast touching the water. Tupper was curiously dispassionate as the water hissed and boiled past the stern, inches from his back. Sure missed that one, he thought. Then as the boat slowly righted, shuddering and shaking, Tupper cleared his head and hauled himself back on board. He stood up, took a stronger grip on the wheel, and with renewed resolve turned the boat and headed once more toward Fastnet Rock.

That was around 1:00 a.m. Tuesday, and *Trophy* was about to go into her death roll.

For more than an hour on *Magistri*, Peter Milligan had been peering at the compass, reading the course, and relaying the information to Peter Cowern or Chris Punter, who in turn shouted it into the ear of Peter Farlinger or Chuck Bentley at the helm. That was the only way they knew they were more or less on the right track. Milligan had been squinting into the wind-driven spray without glasses, a sensation akin to having needles driven through the retina without anesthetic. He could stick his nose right up against the compass, shielding his eyes with his hands, and peer at the compass from an angle, or he could stay low and close and squint. All at once he realized that the red glow of the compass was a blur and he could no longer read the numbers. In fact, he couldn't see anything at all. He had gone blind. "My eyes just ceased to work," Milligan said. "I couldn't get them to focus. I was terrified. The spray was blowing so hard it got into my eyeballs and they short-circuited."

With help, Milligan stumbled below and collapsed at the bottom of the companionway, with his head to the back of the boat. He says it was about as comfortable as lying in a sewer. After a few moments, he rinsed his eyes with fresh water and gradually his sight returned.

The watch had changed. Chuck Bentley handed the helm to Fred Goode, relayed whatever tips on the state of sea he could, and stayed for a while until Goode was comfortable. Goode was in the cockpit with Arch Alyea and Andre Calla. Milligan remembers lying on his back, hearing a deafening crash, being hurled from the floor face first into the cabin roof, and then falling back on the starboard side of the boat. The boat appeared to be upside down, and bodies and gear were lying in a heap of confusion. Blood was running from a cut in his nose, the lights were out, and time was suspended. "I thought we had either been run down by a freighter or hit a rock," Milligan says.

Bentley had wedged himself into an upper berth on the port side. He was thrown out of the bunk and crushed by the weight of falling bodies. Then the pile of men was thrown the opposite way, and he found himself on top.

John Hollidge was at the back of the cabin at his navigation station. When he heard a disembodied voice on deck shout, "Hold on!" he gripped the table and tried to brace himself. At the edge of his vision, bodies were being flung from one side to the other. Hollidge was thrown head first down the back of the stove. He smacked his forehead but was otherwise unhurt. "I think we were ninety degrees, more or less," he says. "I don't think anyone will be able to say with any accuracy, but I ended up going the width of the boat. So it must have been ninety, or thereabouts. It was all over in five seconds at most."

DeGrazia had just closed the hatch and was coming down the companionway when the boat went over. "What flashed through my mind was rocks, but then I thought it can't be rocks, we're in the middle of the damn ocean, for God's sake," he says. "Then I thought maybe it was another boat."

Peter Farlinger, in a detached way, watched himself leave his bunk, brush past the mast, only to end up in a heap on the other bunk. When he struggled free, he found himself standing on the mast. If he were standing on the mast, he thought, then the boat must be horizontal and rolling over. He wondered what was happening to his friends on deck, and that roused him from his detachment. "I thought I would go up and nobody would be there," he says. "I didn't feel panic, but apprehension for Fred and Andre and Arch."

Chris Punter had been half asleep, listening to the wind howling, the halyards slapping against the mast, the hammer blows of the waves. He wasn't comfortable, but it was warm and he was drifting off to sleep. Punter's biggest fears are being run down by a boat in fog or at night, and being trapped inside a sinking boat. He had already met one fear the previous day in the Channel when *Magistri* had narrowly missed the freighter, and now he was about to meet the second. He felt a sense of weightlessness, then the boat fell on its side and stopped. Punter believed they had run into the Dutch destroyer and were being crushed, pinned underneath the ship as it drove over them. His fear, bordering on panic, released a surge of adrenalin, and he threw off the bodies around him and made for the companionway hatch to escape. This was no way to die, he thought, trapped in a small space with the air gradually leaking out, suffocating and finally inhaling and choking on salt water, entombed in a dark, cold grave.

Chuck Bentley had regained his senses, and he got to the hatch first with Punter behind him. Bentley couldn't see the look on Punter's face, or the tightly clenched spoon in Punter's right hand. A little earlier Punter had been eating yogurt and had put the spoon in his pocket. "I was conscious of thinking, 'If this bastard doesn't get out of my way, I'm going to stab him with my spoon because I have to get out of here,'" Punter says.

Punter and Bentley laugh about it now, but at that moment, Punter's fight-or-flight responses had overwhelmed his ability to reason. "I felt panic, because my greatest fear had come to pass," Punter says. "I believed we had been hit by a ship. That's what it felt like. At least that's what I thought getting hit by a ship would feel like."

The big question on Bentley's mind as he opened the hatch was whether there was anybody left on deck.

*Magistri* was steered from a platform on the stern on either side of the tiller. The platform was flat, and normally the helmsman would sit to one side and brace his feet on the other. In light to moderate air, this was quite comfortable. In this storm, there was no way to sit without sliding one way or the other. It was also hard to get enough leverage to move the tiller. It took so much strength to move the rudder that the helmsman was being spelled every twenty minutes, because unlike wheel steering, which has a system of pulleys to distribute the load, tillers are direct drive. "You know what I mean about a fifty-six-pound bag of something?" Hollidge says. "If you keep trying to pick that up and put it down over and over, that's the sort of force we're talking about."

Peter Farlinger, who prided himself on being strong and fit, could barely manage the tiller, and ended up kneeling in the cockpit like a Roman galley slave, pushing and pulling while he braced his back against the bulkhead. Farlinger couldn't see in the dark, so he steered by touch and sound, feeling a Zen-like communion with the boat and elements. "All I could do was feel what the wave was trying to do," he says.

Andre Calla had been feeling as if he had been at a theme park too long. He had been on a roller coaster seemingly forever, feeling stomach-turning fear, weightlessness followed by the G force as the boat drove up a wave. At the top, he says, "You hold your breath because the boat dives and now it's free fall. It's out of control, and you worry about pitch-poling. You're tethered, hanging on to whatever you can, holding on for dear life. The boat is going so fast that it's vibrating."

At the moment of impact, the boat was in a trough. "A valley with mountains on each side," Calla says. As it was swept up the side, Fred Goode screamed, "Big one. Hold on!"

Calla turned and saw a wall of water within arm's length. It was so close he could brush his palm against it, so high that he could not see the top, just the curling foam collapsing. It was alive, he thought, and malignant, and it was moving faster than the boat. Just before it broke, he looked up at the light on top of the mast and saw the foam in reflection: the wave must have been about sixty-five feet tall.

"It came down on top of us like a building collapsing," Calla says. "I was thrown to starboard and completely immersed, holding my breath and feeling like a tadpole in a washing machine, feeling that we were being dragged under the sea. Every part of my body was flailing because of the turbulence. We were buried, the boat went right over, the mast was in the water, the boat was upside down. I was doing a moon walk with an umbilical cord attached."

As Calla's body was being pummelled, his mind was flitting from one thing to the next, adding up the elements that had brought him to this place – the barometer dropping, the sea's rising wind, and the maydays. He wondered if this was the end, believing that the mast would break and crush him. He thought Fred Goode was surely dead, or dying, because of where he had been sitting, opposite the steel traveller, a track that moves the mainsail. Goode must have fallen forward and hit his head on it, or punctured his chest. He was likely now floating unconscious in the water.

"I'm thinking we're going down and that the keel is five tons and I'm attached to the boat going down with it. I'm in darkness, in hell and the womb at the same time. I thought that was it."

Then Calla was caught in a powerful surge of water, and he was back in the boat gasping for breath. Arch Alyea, seeing his friend swept over the side, had grabbed his waist, and both of them had been under water and half out of the boat as it lay down. Alyea says the boat went over when it was at the top of the wave and it rolled past ninety degrees as it slid down, without the mast touching water. That's how high the wave was. He believes they were under for no more than ten seconds before *Magistri* popped up. At the moment of impact, Alyea had been watching the compass. He had had one arm around a stanchion and grabbed Calla with the other. "He wasn't going anywhere," Alyea says. "But I was wondering if we still had a mast. At that point, you didn't know."

Calla's first sights were of Alyea and Goode. Then two hatches on either side of the cockpit popped open and out came Chuck Bentley, Chris Punter, and the rest of the crew.

"We checked the rudder, the shrouds. It was a miracle that the mast was there," Calla says. "It's still blowing seventy-five and you're in the middle of hell, but you're alive."

Fred Goode didn't normally get seasick, but since dinner he had been fighting queasiness. He had been on deck for most of the evening, and been vomiting on and off. He was soaking wet, losing fluids through sweat, and had not been replacing them. Nor was he eating. In those days, sailors ate well, or not at all; provisions did not include high-energy foods such as nuts, chocolate, and dried fruit, items that are standard today. Goode was getting more and more dehydrated, but felt he couldn't go below. "I kept steering because we couldn't afford to lose a driver," he says.

As the adrenalin washed out of his system, it took longer for him to process information, his reaction time slowed, his limbs felt heavy, and his eye-hand coordination deteriorated. He was finding it tough to calculate when to bear off and come back when the waves broke. It was a matter of when, not if something happened. The wave he misjudged sucked the boat under the curl because it was positioned too low as it started the climb up. *Magistri* ended up just where the wave was breaking, and so the boat was pulled into it and then rolled.

"You didn't have much time to think," Goode says. "My main concern was that everyone was holding on because I knew if anybody got washed over our chances of getting them was pretty slim. I hollered to the guys to grab something. We had a traveller system in front of me and I grabbed that. And over we went."

When the boat righted, Goode tried to get his mind to engage his body, but it couldn't. He wondered if the boat was still intact, but couldn't make any effort to find out. Within seconds, Chuck Bentley appeared and yelled across the storm, "What was that? Were we hit?" Bentley saw Goode standing there, the tiller under his arm, not trying to steer. The boat had gone head to wind.

Goode finally asked Bentley where the tiller was. On second glance, it wasn't under Goode's arm but was jammed behind the

Fred Goode was born in Nova Scotia, where he learned to sail at an early age. He was usually *Magistri*'s starting helmsman. (*Arch Alyea*)

backstay. Goode couldn't seem to find it. All he could think about was that Arch Alyea must have been swept away. As his eyes focused, he saw Alyea "wrapped around the coffee grinder, holding on for dear life," Goode says. "We reached down and picked him up. Arch wasn't letting go for anything."

Bentley and Chris Punter realized Goode had gone into shock. He was shivering, staring vacantly, and not doing much of anything. Bentley took the tiller, and the others helped Goode below, stripped off his foul-weather gear, wrapped him in garbage bags to keep him warm, and wedged him into a bunk.

Goode's leg muscles were in a painful knot, and he had stomach cramps that were so severe he wondered if he had pulled a muscle while retching. He tried to rehydrate by drinking water and even came back up later to try steering but couldn't do it. He lay in his bunk until well into the afternoon. Goode says it was the worst part of the race for him because as he lay there in pain, he listened to the radio, which by now was nothing but maydays and messages signalling rescue attempts.

"At that point, I realized how bad it was," Goode says. "It was a horror story. It was a play-by-play and I was right there."

# II

# Small Hours

**"It's not enough that we do our best;**
**sometimes we have to do what's required."**

– WINSTON CHURCHILL

A T ABOUT 3:00 a.m., as *Magistri's* crew struggled to regain its equilibrium after the knockdown, *Evergreen*, though moving in the opposite direction, was facing a similar struggle. The storm was close to its peak, and Ron Barr and Al Megarry were fighting the yacht's tendency to take the path of least resistance and go into the wind, which meant they had to pull on the tiller with all their combined strength until their arms and backs ached. They were sitting on the windward side of the boat, near the stern, feet jammed against the other side of the cockpit. They shouted to each other in short bursts to manage their fear and to reassure themselves that what they were seeing was not an hallucination: green water, writhing and angry, rolling and boiling as it broke under the stern. The wave trains thundered by, and for long seconds at a time it seemed as if there was nothing under them but air.

*Lay off! Lay off!*

The boat surged down into a trough. Whenever *Evergreen* was moving faster than the wave, it would fly off the top like a barrel going over Niagara Falls. For a moment they would feel weightless, before they were thrown forward and came down with a spine-jarring crash.

*Christ! Did you see that?*

Their thoughts were dark and dangerous, nibbling like mice at their will, self-confidence, and self-control.

*Is this it? Is this the one?*

Barr had recently renovated his home and added a deck at the back of the house. It was a pleasant place to sit on a summer evening. He and his wife, Pat, had bought a puppy. It would be a shame, he thought, if he never saw them again or sat on that deck after all the work of building it.

Barr and Megarry weren't really steering, they were running where the wind and waves allowed them to go. They didn't have much control or ability to change direction. Barr estimates *Evergreen* was surfing down the back of the breakers at fourteen to fifteen knots, almost double her hull speed. She was frequently pushed over past horizontal with her keel out of the water. Each time, the violent motion sent them slithering to the length of their tethers, half in and out of the boat.

They had abandoned the watch system, and now it was a case of whoever could, would. Fatigue and hypothermia were taking their toll, and it was imperative each of the crew spent some time out of the wind and rain to rehydrate and warm up. "You were so depleted it was hard to move your body," Barr says. "Your arms and legs wouldn't bend right."

During one break, Al Megarry went below but couldn't sleep. He came back on deck and found Don Green alone at the helm, with his face pressed to the compass. He couldn't read the bearing because he is colour blind and the red light bathing the compass points appeared black to his eyes.

"I said, 'Maybe you should slide over a little and I'll steer,'" Megarry says. "Don was so determined that he did whatever he had to do." But he did relinquish the helm.

Every half a dozen waves or so, a rogue washed over the boat and the man-overboard pole slipped from its tube and was washed into the ocean, running out to the end of its fifty-foot line. To negotiate the eight feet from the front of the cockpit to the stern and retrieve it took five minutes of careful planning. Peter Milligan has likened this sort of task to astronauts preparing for a moon walk. "You have to think through everything you're going to do because if you miss or slip you're gone and there's no way back," he says.

With each breaker, all the loose lines in the cockpit would stream out behind the boat where they risked fouling the propeller. On one retrieval assignment, Barr was swept by a following wave toward the stern, but he managed to grab the mainsheet station before he joined the lines in the sea.

A rogue wave is the one that is most feared, because its motion can't be predicted in conditions that are already taxing the boat and crew to their limits. It tends to be bigger than those that precede it and often moves at a different angle from the rest of the waves. Should it collide with another wave, the combined water forms a super-high breaker. A rogue wave is likely what caused Fred Goode to misjudge the wave that knocked *Magistri* down. It would have been bigger, nastier, and charging at the boat from a different angle. Sailors say that they can hear rogues because they are louder and can be heard above the din of the storm.

Oceanographer William Van Dorn says that on average 5 per cent of waves in a survival storm are rogues, one in twenty. That

Chris Punter adjusts the tension on *Magistri's* jib. (*Andre Calla*)

night, a wave train passed once a minute, so approximately every twenty minutes the fleet was threatened by a rogue, having barely survived the previous nineteen. As Don Green says, "All you can do is concentrate and hang in there."

Green was counting the waves, hoping to anticipate the next big one, but one wave took him by surprise. A wall of water roughly forty feet high overtook *Evergreen*, lifting John Fitzpatrick off the rail and throwing him into the mainsheet winch. Al Megarry felt an impact that was more forceful than diving into a pool and then he was floating. It was over so fast, he didn't know what had happened. He figures that if the mast didn't hit the water, it came close.

The knockdown ripped the stove off its gimbals and sent it bouncing down the length of the cabin, luckily not hitting anyone.

Don Green was thrown under the tiller, across the cockpit, and head first through the lifelines. He was headed into the ocean when his harness jerked him back into the boat. As Megarry climbed back onto the rail, he saw Fitzpatrick clutching his side. His ribs were cracked where he had hit the winch. He went to Fitzpatrick's aid, but there was nothing he could do in the circumstances. Fitzpatrick stayed on deck, keeping his arms wrapped around the lifelines, afraid his body would seize up if he went below to rest.

On some boats, flying gear was also causing injuries. Aboard Richard Nye's forty-eight-foot aluminum-hulled sloop *Carina III*, one crew was injured while making coffee. He was tethered at the galley by a restraining strap, and when the boat lurched, instead of the strap breaking, the wood it was attached to broke away. Drawers were flung open and he was buried under a barrage of cutlery. A carving knife was later found embedded in the door across the way. The worst projectiles were batteries and stoves, the former spilled acid and the later released either propane or highly flammable alcohol. Other objects that went flying were water tanks, spare fuel cans, engine covers, tables, anchors, tool boxes, and gas cylinders.

The crew of the yacht *Valross*, one of sixteen yachts to seek safe haven in Dunmore on the southern coast of Ireland, told how the violent seas threw skipper Tim Bevan head first into a cabin window, smashing it and gashing his head. Bevan told the *Cork Examiner* it was his third Fastnet in the six-year-old boat, and even though he had been an ocean sailor all his life, this was the worst storm he had ever experienced.

Bevan said that, after he picked himself up, with water pouring in the window and through the cockpit hatch, the main electric bilge pump was turned on. It failed, leaving the crew no choice but to bail furiously using a manual pump. A following sea ripped the stove from its base, severing the hose and filling the cabin with propane, choking the crew, until someone shut the tank off. Temporary repairs to the window were ineffective, and every time a big sea broke over the boat, the interior was flooded anew.

"As you lose people's functionality because of fatigue, or injury, or fear, you realize you have another day to go," Steve Killing says. "Then you wonder what's going to happen if there are only two guys left to steer. That's what scared me, the attrition rate."

On *Evergreen*, there was a new worry, whether the rudder would hold. It had been especially built for this Admiral's Cup, and the rudder post, the tube the size of a small gatepost on which the rudder pivots, was made of carbon fibre. The attraction was that it was light as well as strong. As Barr and Megarry worked the tiller, they could feel the post flexing. Thousands of pounds of pressure were being applied to the rudder. Barr wondered how much flexing the post could take before it snapped. As he later learned, all through the fleet, carbon-fibre rudder posts were breaking.

They were the first generation of what has since become standard on racing sailboats, but the prototypes were based solely on mathematical models and stress tests. The Fastnet conditions were well beyond the threshold of normal, and boats of all sizes were finding this out. The Irish suffered most. After the Admiral's Cup races, the Irish team was in the lead and, barring a disaster during the Fastnet race, was expected to win the Cup. Disaster is what befell them, with two of the three boats losing their rudders. Both boats were designed by Ron Holland, both had carbon-fibre rudder posts. The one on the thirty-nine-foot *Regardless* was the first to go at around midnight. *Regardless* was leading the fleet on corrected time and was near the Rock when the post snapped. One of the crew was Gary Carlin, whose Florida firm had built the rudder and others in the race. He later said that the rudders broke when waves picked up the boats and threw them sideways, driving the entire weight of the boat against the post. It's hard to imagine what material could withstand such a blow. *Regardless* was towed by an Irish lifeboat and crew to Baltimore, Ireland.

Next to lose its rudder was the forty-three-foot *Golden Apple of the Sun*, which Ron Holland was crewing. She made it around Fastnet at five minutes after midnight and was headed back to Plymouth early Tuesday when her steering cables jumped off the quadrant. Two hours later, the quadrant was repaired and the boat resumed her course. At 10:00 a.m., a crack was noticed in the rudder, and at 12:45 p.m. with Holland at the helm, the rudder broke off. The crew rigged an emergency tiller from two metal plates and spinnaker poles and hung it over the stern. It snapped immediately.

One boat that lost its rudder rigged an awkward if innovative replacement, by streaming a sail astern. It was tied off to each side of the boat by lines wrapped around winches. When they wanted to go more upwind, they tightened on the windward side and released on the leeward, and when they wanted to go more downwind, they did the reverse. The boat sailed for fifty miles with this rig.

*Golden Apple* was about forty miles west of the Scilly Isles when her rudder broke. Her crew decided to sit it out. On Tuesday afternoon, their radio picked up the news of another severe gale approaching from the west. None of them relished a rerun of the previous night, so when a Wessex helicopter hovered overhead and one of the rescuers radioed, asking, "Are you coming or aren't you?" all ten crew said yes. The last one to leave hung out a sign that read, "Gone for lunch." They returned next day and salvaged the boat.

*Silver Apple of the Moon*, sister ship to *Golden Apple*, was also a Holland design with a carbon-fibre rudder. She was to have been on the Irish team, but failed to race well enough in the trials and had been chartered to the Swiss. She also lost her rudder and was eventually towed to port.

Three Swan 441s – *Quailo, Casse Tete*, and *Big Shadow* – lost their rudders too. In all, half of the fourteen broken rudders in the race were made of carbon fibre. It was the one consistent source of major damage and one of the lessons learned. In an interview with *Newsweek* a few days after the race, Holland admitted that the boat builders did not have enough experience to use carbon fibre properly.

*Evergreen*'s rudder held because of C&C's foresight. Like everyone else, designer Rob Ball didn't know how carbon fibre would behave at the limit. So when he designed the rudder post, he worked out the theoretical maximum load that it might face and then doubled it. Two rudder posts were built and one was load-tested and broke at half the load that the calculation said it should.

"I learned that over the years," says Ball, "you rarely get the numbers the textbook says you will. And that was the perfect example. But because we'd been around a bit, we built in a safety factor that got us through."

*Evergreen* still faced calamity in the small hours of the morning. Killing and Megarry were on deck when a big one came. At the helm, Killing saw the wave coming and realized there was nothing he could do to avoid it. There was no time even for fear, just a sense of inevitability and curiosity about what the collision would be like.

Barr was in a berth at the back end of the boat when it happened. He had crab-walked around *Evergreen*'s hydraulics, past the little galley and the navigation station, moved loose gear out of the way, and crawled into the berth, adjusting the pulleys to stay more or less level. The bilge was a stew of diesel fuel, water, and food, which coated wet sails and clothes with a greasy slick. The boat was leaking from every fitting, and someone was always working the hand pump to take the five or six inches of water down to two. "It was like standing in a gutter in the rain," Barr says.

He didn't bother to strip anything off, just wedged in as he was, soaking wet. He had been there for about fifteen minutes when he felt the boat become airborne and then stop dead with an impact that sent a shudder along the length of the hull. There were groans as fibreglass, steel, and aluminum ground against one another in unintended ways, and Barr and Green heard a loud rushing of water inside the cabin. They believed the hull had split open, the cabin was filling with water, and they were sinking. "I thought we were on our way down, I thought we were gone," Barr says.

Jim Talmage was also below, in a bunk. He interpreted the noises as the mast breaking, and his first instinct was to check where the rod rigging of the mast came through the deck and attached to the chain plate. The rod was still taut, and he was flooded with relief. Green and Barr, overwhelmed by claustrophobia, bounded up the hatch to find Megarry and Killing safe and sound.

Their minds had been playing tricks on them. The shuddering had been real, but the sound of rushing water, which they had interpreted as water rushing in, was the sound of water in the bilge racing forward. Barr was so rattled he would not go below until daylight and even then, he would sleep only at the foot of the companionway ladder.

Fatigue had caught up to Killing, and *Evergreen* had gone off the top of a wave and straight into the next one, instead of taking it at an angle. That had stopped the boat and was the impact everyone had felt. Nothing had broken, and the boat recovered and continued on her way. These were the hours when Killing was most afraid. "We were surviving, but barely," he says.

Ultimately, most of the damage on board *Evergreen* was sustained by humans, not objects. Most of the crew suffered severe seasickness and bumps and bruises that the pitching yacht inflicted. One particularly large wave sent an entire watch off the windward rail and sliding through the cockpit. But while the boat was wet and noisy, it was as strong as an ox. Not a single fitting or fixture broke, the mast stayed up, the rudder bent but didn't break, and the boat everyone thought was the most likely to capsize kept sailing through the night.

On *Magistri*, Fred Goode, half-conscious, was transfixed by radio chatter: the disembodied voices, some in panic, others more measured, making urgent pleas for help, telling of dismasting, injuries, rollovers, crews being swept away. Some men were calmly providing their condition and position, others were hysterical. Goode and John Hollidge listened, relaying messages when they could, their imaginations running wild as the snatches of conversation came and went.

"The guys on deck were lucky they couldn't hear any of it." Goode says. "There were boats the rescuers couldn't get to and then you'd hear, 'That's a body, leave that, and let's try this one.' You could hear that on the VHF."

*Magistri* was close enough to hear the Irish coast guard, which, in coordination with the *Overijssel* and with extraordinary courage in treacherous conditions, was taking sailors off boats or trying to tow disabled vessels to shore. At the height of the storm, the *Overijssel* took water down her stack, which put one engine out of commission. Until it was restarted, there was nothing the destroyer could do but heave to. The acts of the Irish and English coast guards seem all the more heroic set against the paralysis of a war ship.

Goode and Hollidge believed one of the conversations they overheard concerned the rudderless Irish boat *Regardless*. For almost two hours, rescue officials and the boat tried to find one another. "Every two or three minutes, *Regardless* would radio their position and put up a flare. They kept at it and at it," Hollidge says. "I have every respect for those rescue crews. They were out there for thirty-six hours without a break."

Chris Punter, who was also resting below, heard a transmission between *Overijssel* and an unnamed boat.

Boat: We're taking on water and believe we're near you.
*Overijssel*: We can't see you, set off a flare.
Boat: We only have one or two left.
*Overijssel*: We're very close. Let it off.
Boat: Did you see it?
*Overijssel*: No, we didn't.

"It leaves you with a sinking feeling," Punter says, "because it became abundantly clear people were dying."

*Pachena*'s navigator, Pat Leslie, had been below deck all night, frustrated first by the constant error in his course and now by seasickness. Leslie was not usually ill at sea, but between the stress of navigation and the boat's motion, it had crept up on him.

*Pachena* had a good radio and a tall mast and as the coast guard began its rescue operation, Leslie relayed the weaker signals from smaller boats to the *Overijssel* and the *Morningtown*. These signals were picked up by other boats in distress in that area of the Irish Sea, and Leslie's voice was a salve for many in their most fearful moments. Between midnight and 2:00 a.m., when Leslie finally succumbed to seasickness, he was glued to the radio. *Pachena* had charged its two batteries earlier, and Leslie thought he had ample power for the radio. Normal practice is to use one battery to start the engine and the other for lights, radio, and other such needs. This way, there was always one fully charged battery to start the engine and recharge the other. But after Leslie became sick, John Simonett tried to start the engine and couldn't. He realized that the battery selection switch had been left on "Both." The radio had been draining both batteries, and both were almost dead. *Pachena*'s engine was dead and her radio would gradually stop transmitting; for all intents and purposes, she would drop off the face of the Earth. As Steve Tupper puts it, "If something had gone wrong, we would have arrived in Ireland, and not the way we wanted."

The storm's strongest intensity began to be felt around midnight. At that point, it was blowing thirty-five knots at Cork, seventy or so miles northeast of Fastnet. At Fastnet, it was a steady forty, gusting to sixty knots.

Adlard Coles updated *Heavy Weather Sailing* after the race to include a discussion of the 1979 Fastnet storm. He says the violence and chaotic short sea were made far worse by cyclonic gusts that struck in some areas of the course, but not others. This, he says with understatement, was "the main meteorological oddity of this storm." Coles examined the logs of as many boats as he could, to look at the barometric pressures they had recorded, as well as the state of the wind and sea. His conclusion was that wind speeds varied by twenty or more knots within a few miles.

Chuck Bentley is convinced that *Magistri* survived gusts of

eighty-five knots, which would fit what Coles found. "Our anemo-
meter was nailed shut at sixty," Bentley says. "It wasn't moving. I'm
sure we saw a hundred-mile-an-hour winds and forty-five-foot-
plus seas." Others corroborate the height of the waves, estimating
them at between forty and fifty feet as measured against the tops of
their mast or the height of the spreaders. Steve Killing, noting the
tendency of sailors to exaggerate, believes there were gusts of seventy
knots, but waves only of thirty feet. "Take all the estimates and mul-
tiply by 80 per cent and you'll be about right," he says. Steve Tupper
figures the tallest waves were fifty feet high. "I must stress it was not
the worst race I have been it," he says. "It was just the most famous.
But where we were, it was blowing like hell."

When Doug Race later read accounts of the race, it was driven
home to him how much conditions varied. The big boats such as
Ted Turner's *Tenacious* and John Rousmaniere's *Toscana* were sailing
away from the storm in forty and fifty knots while *Pachena* was
facing winds in the low sixties. Race later spoke to Rob James, who
was aboard *Condor of Bermuda*. James said the wind was forty knots
in the Channel and they were flying a spinnaker, "racing full on,"
at the same time *Pachena* was struggling for its life.

The differences in wind intensity weren't the only meteorological oddity. At 10:30 p.m. Monday, the thirty-four-foot *Moonstone*
saw low clouds moving over the boat from east to west at a speed
of twenty to thirty knots, while wind was blowing thirty-five knots
from the opposite direction. *Moonstone*'s navigator, an experienced
ocean-racing man, told Coles he had never seen anything like it in
all his time at sea.

A wind speed of thirty-five knots in one direction encounter-
ing twenty blowing the other way is fifty-five knots at the point of
impact. Coles suggests the only way to explain this is if a stationary

vortex of wind not far above the surface funnelled these winds downward. That would create short, steep seas with an unusually small wave length.

"The problem was not the wind, it was the sea," Doug Race says. "They were steep and confused, not like the rollers you get offshore. It was the seas that did it to you. The seas were crashing on deck, breaking glass, crashing in hatches, rolling boats, and knocking people overboard. The wind was incidental."

Those downward gusts of wind, which Adlard Coles calls "jets," likely combined with the gale-force winds at the centre of the storm to create mean speeds of fifty-five knots with gusts to sixty-five or more. The strange seas were then sustained by winds that veered almost ninety degrees and by gusts and squalls coming from several directions. British meteorologist Alan Watts called this effect "the most potent feature of the tragedy."

The strongest winds were first experienced near Fastnet Rock and moved south. The German Admiral's Cup boat *Jan Pott* recorded fifty knots at midnight when she was approaching the Rock, not far from *Magistri* and *Pachena*. At 6:30 a.m., after rounding Fastnet and covering thirty miles of the return leg, *Pott* was rolled through 360 degrees. *Magistri* had just rounded the lighthouse at that point and her wind speed indicator was stuck on sixty. As the storm centre moved south, it overtook the smallest boats and lesser-experienced crews just before dawn as they struggled upwind. *Evergreen* would have been near the centre at this time, though in the better position of moving away from it, not toward it.

Many of the boats sailed through the eye of the storm, under a clear night sky with stars and a bright moon. On *Pachena*, they reckoned the eye passed over at about 2:00 a.m. They were enormously relieved because for the first time in hours the wind dropped and they weren't shouting over it to be heard, even though the waves were huge. As *Magistri* scratched her way to Fastnet after her knock-down, Peter Cowern felt the same reprieve as the wind died and the moon came out. "I thought, This is great, it's all finished," he says. "Then I realized we were just in the middle of it and there was more to come."

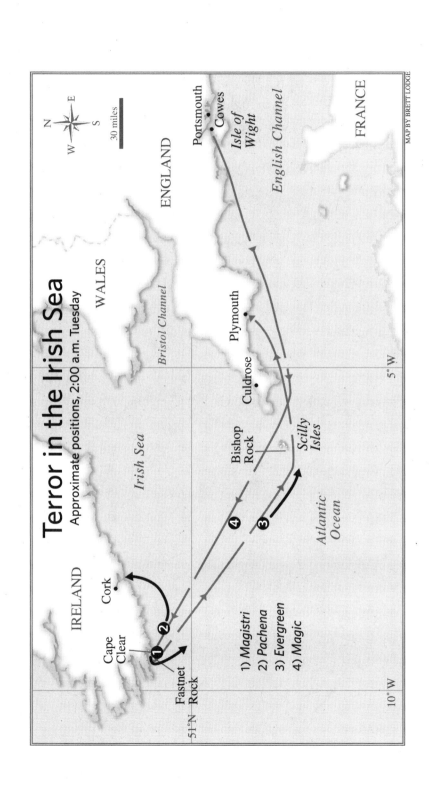

# Terror in the Irish Sea

Approximate positions, 2:00 a.m. Tuesday

IRELAND

Cork

Cape
Clear

Fastnet
Rock

51°N

10°W

Irish Sea

WALES

Bristol Channel

ENGLAND

Portsmouth

Cowes

Isle of
Wight

English Channel

Plymouth

Culdrose

Bishop
Rock

Scilly
Isles

Atlantic
Ocean

FRANCE

5°W

1) Magistri
2) Pachena
3) Evergreen
4) Magic

① ② ③ ④

N
W E
S

30 miles

MAP BY BRETT LODGE

# 12

## *Mayday*

**"Courage is almost a contradiction in terms. It means a strong desire to live taking the form of readiness to die."**

— G.K. CHESTERTON

By 2:00 A.M. on Tuesday, August 14, the Fastnet fleet was in a shambles, and the dream that had drawn the 303 boats to the starting line was no longer a challenge, or even an exhilarating ride, but an unfolding tragedy. Some crews had deluded themselves by thinking that the weather would improve and that running for shelter was more dangerous than continuing on. Others had tried to run, but discovered it was too late. Boats were being swamped and were capsizing and rolling through 360 degrees. Crews were in shock or being swept overboard or trapped underneath overturned yachts. Some had taken down all sail; others were flying a little. Many were down below with their hatches shut tight, hoping they could wait it out. Former British prime minister Ted Heath, a veteran of several decades of political life and thousands of miles of ocean sailing, later said, "It was the worst experience of my life."

This wasn't bad weather, it wasn't rough weather, it was a killer storm. Search-and-rescue officials couldn't launch a quick and effective response because the fleet was so large and spread out. Compounding the problem was that it was the middle of the summer and only a skeleton crew was on hand. And since only Admiral's Cup boats were required to have two-way radios, the precise location of many boats was unknown.

The 1979 fleet was the largest ever, capping a decade-long resurgence in sailing that had been inspired by a new generation of heroes and the widespread introduction of fibreglass as a boat-building material. The former was a reason to go sailing, the latter provided the means, for it dramatically reduced the cost of ownership.

Sir Francis Chichester was the first of the sailing heroes to capture the popular imagination. The aircraft designer and pilot had come to public attention in 1960 when he won the first Single-handed Trans-Atlantic Race, later to be sponsored by the *Observer* newspaper and renamed the OSTAR. The race had been proposed in 1956 by a retired British officer, Col. "Blondie" Hasler, who liked dangerous things and wanted a competition that would take boats and owners to the edge. It didn't get off the ground until 1960 when Hasler, Chichester, and three others set off with very little fanfare to compete against one another and the sea. Chichester, then fifty-eight, was recovering from lung-cancer surgery but went on to win the inaugural race in the thirty-nine-foot *Gypsy Moth III*. He followed up this achievement with a series of inspirational books about his sailing adventures that made him famous.

In the 1964 OSTAR, Chichester came second to a young Frenchman called Eric Tabarly, who went on to inspire a generation of French sailors. By then, Chichester had had enough of sailing back and forth "across the pond" and had moved on to a larger goal, the ultimate one for single-handers: sailing around Cape Horn.

His new fifty-four-foot *Gypsy Moth IV* left Plymouth in August 1966 and returned the following May. He rounded the Cape of Good Hope and made one stop in Sydney, Australia. The adventure captivated the public and his exploits were well covered. On his return, Chichester was greeted by an enormous crowd, given a knighthood, and became an emblem of the can-do British spirit. He embodied the things that had once made Britain great: perseverance, pluck, courage in the face of adversity, success in the face of enormous odds. His voyage was followed a year later by greengrocer Alec Rose, who circumnavigated in his thirty-six-foot *Lively Lady*. He, too, was knighted.

In the meantime, Chichester upped the ante, declaring that the only challenge left for single-handers was a *non-stop* circumnavigation. It was seen then as an almost impossible achievement, but in early 1968, London's *Sunday Times* put up a £5,000 prize and a trophy called the Golden Globe. The race was on.

Nine mariners set sail in the 1968 Golden Globe race. Only three rounded the Horn and only one finished. He was Robin Knox-Johnston, a merchant seaman who made the voyage in 312 days. Knox-Johnston had no idea he had won until he tied up in Plymouth. His radio had broken some weeks earlier, but as the third Briton in three years to circumnavigate the world, he was made a Commander of the British Empire (CBE) and later knighted. Other sailors followed, including Rob James, sailing this Fastnet aboard *Condor of Bermuda*. Single-handing made Britain feel good again. Enthusiasts like Ted Heath lent enormous cachet to the sport. Throughout the 1970s, Heath was a fixture of the British Admiral's Cup team and led it to victory in 1971. In 1973, while prime minister, he flew home from a meeting of Commonwealth first ministers in Ottawa to be on his boat for the start of the Fastnet race.

Soon, other races were added to the sailing calendar, including the first of the Around the World races jointly sponsored by Whitbread and the Royal Naval Sailing Association. What became known as the Whitbread was first run in 1971 and attracted 17 boats and 167 crew. Whitbread continued to sponsor the race for thirty years, until it was taken over by automaker Volvo. In the meantime, the popularity of the Fastnet grew, for this was a chance for the Sunday sailors to race alongside serious players. For Europeans, it was close to home, took only four to six days, and offered a taste of the open ocean but with less peril.

The sport's resurgence was not confined to Europe. In the United States in 1979, Catalina Yachts and Hunter Yachts were celebrating their tenth anniversaries. A decade earlier they had been building twenty-two-foot daysailers, now the lines of their cruising yachts stretched into the thirty- to forty-foot range. In Canada, builders included Tanzer, CS, Mirage, Hughes, Grampian, Aloha, Hinterhoeller, Nonsuch, and Bayfield. But it was C&C Yachts that was widely considered to be Canada's premier builder, for the quality rather than the quantity of boats it produced. C&C had carefully turned its racing successes into industry fame, and so it was often mentioned in the same breath as the large American builders. Business was so good that C&C opened a plant in Rhode Island in 1976 and another in Kiel, West Germany, in 1978. It saw itself as an international force.

As the storms converged on the 1979 fleet, the casualties were largely among the two hundred smaller non-Admiral's Cup boats. They were still heading toward the Fastnet as the bigger boats were coming back. Fifteen of the men who died were on boats less than thirty-eight feet long. The two others who died were aboard a thirty-eight-foot trimaran called *Buck's Fizz*, which was following the race but not participating in it. The boat was found floating upside down with none of the four crew inside. Two bodies were recovered, but the other two were never found.

Eighteen of the nineteen abandoned boats were also from this group of smaller boats. The nineteenth was *Golden Apple of the Sun*, the Admiral's Cup yacht that lost her rudder.

The crews of these boats were not as experienced at ocean racing as those on the larger yachts, but most had done some ocean racing, had plenty of inshore experience, and knew how to handle their boats when the going got tough. They also had the proper safety equipment. Some of those who got into the worst trouble made the wrong decisions, but most were just incredibly unlucky, caught at the wrong moment by the same big wave that others were able to avoid.

Frank Halliday "Hal" Ferris, the skipper of the American yacht *Ariadne*, typified the weekenders who wanted a taste of the big time. Before moving to England, Ferris had worked for eight years in Toronto as an executive of Federal Pioneer Ltd., a manufacturer of electrical distribution equipment. While in Toronto, Ferris raced Star and Dragon class boats at the Royal Canadian Yacht Club. A competitive man, he took up ocean racing in 1974 when he was transferred to Wolverhampton, England, to work with a subsidiary of the company. Not long after he arrived, Ferris bought *Ariadne*, a thirty-five-foot wooden boat. He was sixty-one at the time of the race. During his five years in Britain, he had acquired considerable experience sailing both inshore and offshore, honing his skills in many races, including the Solent during Cowes Race Week. Ferris had spent the spring and summer of 1979 doing work-up Royal Ocean Racing Club events, giving his crew experience and a degree of comfort with the boat. There were five others aboard for the Fastnet, with differing levels of skill. *Ariadne* was not especially vulnerable compared with the other boats, but the misadventure that befell her was out of all proportion to what should have happened. It led John Rousmaniere to describe her as the unluckiest boat in the world.

On Monday afternoon as the wind increased, *Ariadne* was sailing straight toward the Fastnet with her largest jib. The crew gradually reduced sail, donned weather gear, clipped on safety harnesses, and hunkered down for a wet night. At about 10:00 p.m., they reefed the mainsail and changed down to a smaller jib. Not long after, they reefed again. Then the mainsail split and was taken down completely.

Just after midnight, with the wind speed instrument reading sixty knots and the BBC forecast calling for Force 10, Ferris called it quits. He was about twenty-four miles to the northeast of *Evergreen*, which had turned back two hours earlier and was coming to the aid of *Magic*. *Evergreen* was flying her storm jib and had a small piece of her mainsail up. She was able to carry this much sail because she was running downwind, rather than beating into its full force. It is also possible her rebuilt keel with its heavy steel plate made the boat more stable, if somewhat slower. To this point, the *Ariadne* crew had done everything right – steadily reduced sail, battened down, donned safety harnesses and life jackets – and had calmly gone about the business of sailing the boat.

After the decision was made to quit, and before *Ariadne* turned around, the crew changed the number-three jib for the smaller number four. Ferris eased the boat off on a reach, planning to make for Ireland, which lay to the northeast. He found that even that small amount of sail was too much and replaced the number four with the storm jib.

At 2:00 a.m., *Ariadne*'s storm jib ripped and now she ran before the wind under bare poles. To make the boat more manageable, the torn sail was tied to lines and streamed from the stern to keep the boat angled to the waves and to slow her down. On board *Magic*, they had also tried this. Both ends of about two hundred feet of rope had been tied to cleats on either side of the boat, so that a long loop trailed overboard. According to the theory, the resistance created by the rope would slow the boat, and steady its motion by bringing the stern into the waves. Instead, the motion became worse as waves drove under the stern and pitched the boat up and down, just as she was being knocked from side to side. It was nauseating, so *Magic* hauled the line in and found the motion much improved. *Ariadne* left hers out.

Around the same time as Fred Goode misjudged the wave that knocked *Magistri* past horizontal, David Crisp at *Ariadne*'s helm made the same mistake but with far more serious consequences. Perhaps the rogue wave was bigger, or *Magistri* was that much heavier, but Crisp's misjudgment meant the boat kept rolling until her keel was in the air and her mast was pointing to the ocean floor. Both Crisp and Rob Gilders, who was in the cockpit with him, were thrown into the ocean to the length of their tethers. A death spiral of events was now in motion.

Crisp was trapped underneath the boat, and as it righted itself he was able to climb back in. So was Gilders. Down below in the cabin, forty-three-year-old Bill LeFevre had gashed his head on something sharp. He was woozy and bleeding profusely. His wound was tended to as best as possible. The three others with him were fine, although the water in the cabin was waist deep. The hatch covers were smashed. The crew bailed furiously with pots and buckets and lowered the water by a foot or so. On deck, the mast was broken in several pieces and tangled with the wire rigging and was swinging like a marionette, first this way, then that.

Despite being rolled at least twice and dismasted – and
abandoned by her crew – *Ariadne* did not sink. (*Royal Navy*)

*Ariadne* was low in the water, sluggish, and without the benefit
of a mast to counteract the force of the keel. She swung violently,
but the crew kept their heads and continued to bail. By 5:30 a.m.,
it was getting light, the cabin had been pumped out, and although
the boat was a mess, they thought they could jury-rig a mast and,
when the seas subsided, limp to shore.

Then *Ariadne* was caught by a wave and rolled through 360
degrees. Once again, David Crisp was thrown into the sea and jerked
short at the end of his tether. He was able to swim back. Bob Robie,
a sixty-three-year-old American oil company executive, wasn't so
lucky. It is unclear whether his tether snapped or the fixture to which
it was attached broke. Crisp saw him surface about fifty yards from
the boat. They waved to each other, and Robie was never seen again.

The crew was convinced that *Ariadne* was about to sink. The
cabin was almost full of water and there was just a few inches of

freeboard. Another rollover seemed imminent. At about 6:00 a.m., Ferris decided to abandon ship. They inflated the life raft and dropped it over the side. Bill LeFevre was helped in, and the four others climbed in and cut the raft loose. Everything was done by the book. They watched the boat drift away.

At about 8:00 a.m., one of the crew stuck his head out of the raft and saw a freighter a few hundred yards away. It was a German boat called the *Nanna*. At that moment, the raft capsized, possibly because of the turbulence caused by the boat, or because the men all shifted weight suddenly. As the freighter drew alongside, Rob Gilders managed to grab the rung of the ship's ladder and pull himself up. Ferris tried next. He unhooked himself from the raft, plunged into the water, grabbed for the ladder, but missed. He was swept away and did not have the strength to swim back.

The freighter made two more passes, but only one of the three men left in the raft, Matthew Hunt, managed to climb up. A second made the ladder but was still hooked to the raft and when the raft was jerked by a wave, he fell back into the sea and was gone. LeFevre was alone in the raft.

About five hours later, Frank Ferris was spotted floating in the water and rescued by helicopter. The helicopter had been trying to find *Ariadne*, but had come across *Magic* first, rescued her crew, and taken them to the Royal Naval Air Station in Culdrose, Cornwall. On the return trip, it spotted Ferris bobbing in the ocean. He was still alive when he was rescued, but died en route to hospital. The bodies of the other two crew were never found. *Ariadne* did not sink. She remained afloat, was recovered, and towed to Penzance in Cornwall. Her loss of life was the greatest of all the boats in the race.

Frank Ferris had been in the water for five hours but was still alive when this picture was taken during his rescue. He died en route to hospital. (*Royal Navy*)

The crew of the thirty-two-foot *Gunslinger* thought that they were prepared too. Late Monday evening, they changed down to a storm jib and, like *Ariadne*, ran before the storm. Shortly before making that decision, *Gunslinger* had beat to windward for thirty minutes to help another yacht in distress. After that ordeal, skipper Robert Lloyd, a forty-nine-year-old London banker, decided that if the seas got worse they would drop the storm jib and wait it out. They did get worse, so *Gunslinger* dropped her jib and for some time lay ahull, drifting with no sail up and her rudder lashed hard over. But the motion wasn't comfortable, so Lloyd decided to run off. All was fine for two hours, then without warning "the rudder snapped like a carrot," Lloyd says. Freed from all restraining force, *Gunslinger* started to round up and head into the wind. At that moment, she slid off the top of a wave and was slammed onto her side. Lloyd was thrown to the end of his tether. The boat popped up, he crawled back in, and another wave hit. This time the boat was rolled through 360 degrees. She righted again, but the cabin was knee deep in water and more seemed to be coming in. When it rose to waist high, one crew used the radio to issue a mayday, while another readied the life raft. It was inflated and tied to the side of the boat. Again, there was no panic, just an orderly retreat.

Paul Baldwin went into the raft first and was handed flashlights, flares, and food. At that moment a third wave struck, flipping the raft and trapping the thirty-year-old Baldwin underneath. He was wearing a life jacket and struggled to swim free. He hadn't quite made it when the rope attaching the raft to the boat broke. Both the raft and Baldwin were swept away. The remaining crew had no means of escape and turned their efforts to saving the boat. They gradually gained on the water and concluded she wasn't leaking but was filling up from water that had accumulated in her lockers. On Tuesday afternoon, a helicopter airlifted one crewman who had injured his hand during the launch of the raft. The rest of the crew waited until Wednesday when a Dutch trawler towed them to Crosshaven, where they arrived midday. *Gunslinger's* only damage was the broken rudder. Paul Baldwin's body was found two days later.

Despite the tragedy, Robert Lloyd defended the actions of his crew and dismissed the broader criticism that many of the smaller boats were too light and unstable. "I've got nothing but praise for *Gunslinger*," he told *Newsweek*. "It's extraordinarily seaworthy. You can say we lost one man. You can also say that five men were saved. It was the boat that saved them, not the safety equipment."

The crew of *Grimalkin*, a thirty-foot fibreglass boat skippered by David Sheahan, an accountant in his forties, also thought they were doing things right. By 11:00 p.m. Monday, *Grimalkin* was down to a storm jib. All six men stayed in the cockpit, including

This photograph of
*Grimalkin* was taken
from a Royal Navy
helicopter. Three crew
members had abandoned
the boat, leaving two
others aboard, one of
whom later died.
*(Royal Navy)*

Sheahan's seventeen-year-old son Matthew. All had safety harnesses
on. By 3:00 a.m., they were down to bare poles and running, trailing hundreds of feet of rope behind them. In the next two hours,
*Grimalkin* was knocked down until her mast touched the water
about half a dozen times and all six men were thrown overboard
each time. Each time they crawled back in, a little more tired and
a little more hypothermic. At about 5:00 a.m., they had had enough
and *Grimalkin* radioed a mayday. Not long afterwards, she was

knocked down and this time did a full rotation. As she lay upside down, Sheahan was trapped underneath the boat, and to free him, the crew cut his tether. When she righted he drifted away, unable to get back in the boat. His body was never found. With the mast shattered and the cabin awash, three of the men, including Matthew Sheahan, inflated the life raft and cast off. After several terrifying hours, they were rescued by helicopter. They had abandoned two injured and unconscious crew who were buried under debris, one of whom died. The other was later rescued by helicopter. *Grimalkin* didn't sink and was towed ashore.

Such catastrophes were happening all through Monday night and into the next day, some worse than others. On *Festina Tertia*, disaster struck Tuesday afternoon at about 1:30 p.m. when the worst of the wind had passed but the waves were still enormous. As reported by the *Los Angeles Times*, the thirty-five-footer had rounded Fastnet and was on the way back to Plymouth. She had abandoned the race and was sailing well under storm jib on a reach. The only damage had been to the boom, which had broken during the night.

Sean Thrower, thirty, one of eight aboard, was asleep after having been on deck most of the night when he felt the boat swing around. He went up to see a wave about forty feet high. The sun was out and it glistened off the foam on top, which made it all the more frightening to him. The wave broke and his friend Roger Watts was washed overboard. The crew started man-overboard procedures, turning the boat around while one man pointed and kept his eyes fixed on the floating figure of Watts. When they got close to Watts, who was face down in the water, Thrower was so frantic he stripped off his foul-weather jacket and pants as well as his boots and with a rope in his hand jumped into the water, swimming hard toward his friend. On board, they were shouting at him to come back.

"Somebody said, 'It's no good,'" Thrower said. "He is floating in the water with his face down. He is clearly dead." Watts's body drifted away, and back aboard *Festina Tertia*, Thrower seemed to be hypothermic and going into shock. His mates radioed a mayday, and Thrower was picked up by helicopter and taken to RNAS Culdrose.

Aboard *Flashlight*, two more men died. Russell Brown and Charles Stevenson were both young British naval officers, sailing on a thirty-five-foot boat owned by the Royal Naval Engineering College in Plymouth. Like many other boats, *Flashlight* was rolled by a rogue wave and both men on deck were thrown into the sea. Both were clipped on with safety harnesses, but both harnesses broke, in different places.

These two deaths are what still stand out most clearly in the mind of *Magistri's* navigator, John Hollidge. "I had taught both of them to sail," he says. "Sadly, they were never seen again."

On the Dutch boat *Veronier II*, a man was lost in a similar way. It was suspected the shock overload of his weight on the harness's webbing made it snap. Peter Dorey, a senior politician from the Channel Island of Guernsey, drowned after being swept overhead from his thirty-seven-foot yacht *Cavale*. Dorey, fifty-one, was the head of a shipping company and president of the Guernsey's Advisory and Finance Committee, effectively the finance minister.

On other boats, disaster did not end in tragedy. Some of the worst accidents resulted from 360-degree rolls. The largest to be bowled over this way was the forty-six-foot German boat *Jan Pott*. Olympic silver and bronze medallist Ulli Libor was at the helm and managed to hang on to the wheel throughout that roll. Down below, a resting crewman had some teeth knocked out. The boat lost her rig, but otherwise remained intact. The crew jury-rigged a spinnaker pole for a mast and initially used a sail bag as a storm jib, which was more than enough sail. They later replaced it with a small

A Royal Navy Wessex
helicopter hovers over
the *Camargue* during
the resuce of her crew.
(*Royal Navy*)

jib, with the foot set as a luff. The boat made it safely to Plymouth.

The thirty-six-foot *Tiderace* did a full roll while running with bare poles. Her mast broke, two of her crew were swept overboard, and the lifeline of one of the two snapped. He waved frantically from a wave top and somehow managed to catch a line hurled to him.

The *Camargue*, a thirty-four-foot English boat, was smashed by a wave at about 8:45 a.m. Tuesday, throwing all the men on deck overboard. Two were rolled back by the same wave, while a third was left tangled in the lifelines at the stern. The skipper, Arthur

Moss, was thrown to the length of his tether. Moss sent out a mayday, and when the helicopter arrived, he pushed his crew into the ocean one by one so they could swim away from the ship and be rescued by helicopter. Moss later said, "I never thought I would see a steering wheel, complete with a man attached, soar into the seas. Thank God for our life ropes." *Camargue* didn't sink either and was later retrieved intact.

Ted Heath was shaken when *Morning Cloud* was knocked over more than ninety degrees. *Morning Cloud* had rounded Fastnet at about 1:30 a.m., and at about 4:00 a.m., as *Magistri* was about to round the rock, a rogue wave overtook her and rolled her well past ninety degrees but not quite upside down. The helmsman was thrown so hard against the wheel he dented it. Heath was below and thrown across the cabin. When the boat righted itself, the crew was so shaken that they took down all sail and lay ahull for several hours, perhaps fearing that the rudder would break, which had already happened earlier, during the cross-Channel race.

Helicopters rescued one man near the dismasted French yacht *Tarantula*. *Polar Bear* was pitch-poled. This thirty-three-footer had seen the same flare as *Trophy* and gone to the aid of *Allemander*. *Polar Bear*'s skipper was fifty-year-old Maj. John Moreton of the Queen's Dragoon Guards, an experienced sailor, whose crew of five included his wife, Brigid. As they moved toward the distressed yacht, *Polar Bear* was pitch-poled and somersaulted end over end. The impact broke Brigid Moreton's arm, tore away the mast, and ripped off a piece of the deck. The crew, which included three young officers from the Dragoon Guards, launched their lifeboat. It overturned, but they managed to right it and get back in. They were the first survivors to be picked up by the *Overijssel*.

Major Moreton later said that the Dutch destroyer was rolling so badly they could almost step on to her deck as it rolled to sea level. Brigid Moreton's arm was set by the ship's doctor. Badly damaged though she was, *Polar Bear* didn't sink and was later salvaged by Cornish fishermen.

The forty-two-foot *Lancer* was rolled well below horizontal, even though she wasn't carrying a stitch of sail. Those below were injured by the impact, including the owner, whose face was gashed.

The thirty-three-footer *Gringo*, skippered by Richard Milward, was knocked flat three times. The first time her mast was damaged; two hours later she was knocked down again but still survived. The third time she was flattened, she was dismasted and her coach roof was stoved in. All seven of her crew took to the life raft, where they waited six hours for rescue. Milward insisted on a watch-keeping and sleeping rotation as the huge cresting seas made life on board the raft almost unbearable. The waves kept breaking over the raft and the seven men were constantly bailing. At one point, the skipper and crewman Adrien Hammond were thrown overboard. Milward was washed back aboard, but Hammond suffered rib injuries and had to be hauled back in.

In all, twenty-four boats were abandoned, of which nineteen were recovered. Of the five that sunk, one was under tow.

There were many heroic acts by boats coming to the rescue of others in distress. The *Griffin*, operated by Royal Ocean Racing Club, had three staff instructors on board, including skipper Stewart Quarrie and four students. In the dark, Quarrie took two bad waves and behind them an enormous one with the top fifteen feet or so vertical. He shouted to the others in the cockpit to hang on and then he was thrown into the water.

*Griffin* was rolled until her mast pointed to the ocean floor and remained upside down for at least half a minute. The impact shattered the mast. Quarrie was thrown out of the boat with such force that the hook on the end of his harness was bent straight. Two others were trapped under the boat but managed to unhook themselves and swim out. Inside the boat, one of the hatch boards was missing, and the four other crewmen agonized as water filled the cabin. Slowly the boat righted and with only a few inches of freeboard remaining, the crew hauled out the life raft and made ready to abandon ship. One of the students bravely dived into the cabin to retrieve flares, and when he returned they cut the raft free.

About forty-five minutes later, the raft capsized. Somehow the crew managed to right it and clamber back aboard, but in righting it they demolished the canopy, adding hypothermia to their problems. One crewman had been changing into dry clothes when the wave hit and was wearing only a T-shirt and pants. Then someone spotted a light in the distance and they fired a parachute flare and then another. One of these caught the eye of the crew of the thirty-six-foot French yacht *Lorrelei*, skippered by Alain Catherineau. Catherineau turned his boat to come to their aid, but it was half an hour before he came alongside. After several passes, he recovered all seven *Griffin* crew. The crewman in the T-shirt was so hypothermic he could not get himself onto the boat and had to be hauled aboard. At one point during the rescue, *Lorrelei* was knocked flat.

For the rest of the day, with thirteen people on board, *Lorrelei* lay ahull, riding out the storm. When the wind moderated, she sailed for Plymouth. *Griffin* eventually sank, the broken hatch allowing her to fill up. For her efforts, *Lorrelei* was awarded second equal place in Class IV, and her skipper was named Yachtsman of the Year by the British Yachting Journalists' Association for his outstanding seamanship and bravery.

The second rescue by a yacht was when the Royal Navy's *Dasher* came to the aid of the thirty-two-foot French yacht *Maligawa III*. The fifty-five-foot *Dasher* had abandoned the race early Tuesday morning and was running with a reefed mainsail. At about 4:30 a.m., the helmsman notified the skipper that he had heard a cry. With a powerful flashlight, they saw a boat quite close by. She was dismasted, the windows on one side were smashed in, and she had no running lights on. *Dasher* managed to heave a line to the boat and took her in tow. After about half an hour, a wave caught the crippled boat and rolled her past horizontal, throwing two crew into the sea. They had had enough and launched their raft. *Dasher* made several passes back and forth and pulled all six crew off the raft. *Maligawa III* later sunk.

*Moonstone*, the thirty-four-footer that earlier reported seeing clouds moving in the opposite direction to the wind, was the third yacht to come to the rescue of another boat. The mast of the French yacht *Alvena* had been bent in one knockdown and a subsequent broach swept it away entirely, leaving a hole in the deck. The cabin quickly filled with water, and the crew believed she was in imminent danger of sinking. They abandoned ship at about 6:00 a.m. Five hours later, *Moonstone* came across the raft, which in the meantime had overturned twice. *Moonstone* had been hove to for part of the night with her storm jib sheeted tightly to windward and her tiller locked to leeward. She had been knocked horizontal twice.

*Moonstone* turned on her engine but couldn't safely come alongside the raft. Eventually she hove to to windward, tied a line to a life ring, and floated it down to the raft, just what *Evergreen* had tried for *Magic*. *Alvena*'s crew caught the life ring and fastened the line to the raft. It took three crewman on *Moonstone* to pull it alongside. The rescue took only thirty minutes. *Alvena*, in spite of her crew's conviction that they had seen her sink, was later towed into Cork.

By early Tuesday morning, the British search-and-rescue network had been roused from a midsummer slumber to cope with the worst maritime disaster since the end of the Second World War. For three and a half days, eight helicopters, six naval vessels, and dozens of commercial ships ranged more than twenty thousand square miles of ocean and rescued 136 people who might otherwise have perished. The mobilization began just before dawn Tuesday when the Officer of the Day at the Royal Navy Air Service base at Culdrose, Cornwall, was awoken by a call. He was told that two incidents had occurred in the Fastnet race.

The first was that *Magic* was rudderless and drifting about fifty-five miles northwest of Land's End, or about seventy-two miles from the base. The second was that a raft with four people on board (Frank Ferris's crew from *Ariadne*) had been spotted about forty miles farther up the course. The Southern Rescue Co-ordination Centre, Plymouth, which was receiving these distress calls, requested help from the Navy. Culdrose had two Wessex helicopters with a range of 120 nautical miles – one of which picked up *Magic's* mayday – and two longer-range Westland Sea Kings with a range roughly double that of the Wessex. The Sea Kings could fly at night in all weather, while the Wessex helicopters were confined to operating in daylight. The Sea Kings had a crew of four: two pilots and two others who were either the winch operator or rescuer, depending on the circumstances. The Wessex had one pilot, one winch operator, and one diver. Within the hour, two Wessex helicopters were airborne, and by dawn the wider alarm brought in Navy tugs and aircraft from as far away as Scotland.

As the morning wore on, it was clear more help was needed. Although it was the first week of summer leave, leaving the base short-staffed, Culdrose was able to mobilize volunteer crews. Squadrons at Prestwick in Scotland and at Yeovilton in Somerset also pitched in. Helicopters from Culdrose flew two hundred hours collectively, and many hours were put in by fighter jets from the Royal Air Force base at St. Mawgan in Cornwall. Lifeboats at all points in Cornwall and the south coast of Ireland were involved. The *Overijssel* was joined by the British fishery protection vessel HMS *Anglesey* and the frigate HMS *Broadsword*. The *Broadsword* was supported by two naval tugs, *Rollicker* and *Robust*.

By the end of the first day, seventy-five people from seventeen boats had been rescued, and most of them passed through Culdrose like guests at a wedding receiving line. They came in wet and exhausted, were given hot baths, a drink, and a place to nap while their clothes were laundered. Then they were shuffled out the back door onto a bus to Plymouth to make room for the incoming.

The helicopter rescues were fraught with danger. As the boats wallowed in the high sea, the masts whipped back and forth, threatening to tangle the divers and their cables. This was why the crews were instructed to jump into the water and let their boats drift away. Only then would the diver drop down and swim to them. It was terrifying.

"That was the hairiest part of all," said Frank Worsley of *Camargue*. "The idea of jumping into those huge seas was appalling. In the end, we were all pushed in by the skipper. When it was his turn, it took him a good long time to make the jump."

# 13

# *Fastnet Rock*

**"Do not dwell in the past, do not dream of the future,
concentrate the mind on the present moment."**

– PRINCE SIDDHARTA

WITH FRED GOODE tucked safely below and *Magistri* under
control, Chuck Bentley took stock. Keep racing or turn and run?
It was about 2:00 a.m. Tuesday and the Fastnet light was just four
miles or so upwind. As *Magistri* rose and fell on waves, the crew
could see its powerful light blinking. If they continued and rounded
the rock, they would be able to bear off, as *Evergreen* had done hours
earlier, sailing a more manageable downwind course for Plymouth.
They wouldn't be home free, but it would certainly be a more comfortable ride. The question was whether they could get around
Fastnet without injury or damage. The only other option was to turn
around, but this would mean they were disqualified from the race.

Death was a close companion now and had been since the
knockdown. The crew had passed into a realm of sensory chaos.
They had glimpsed a place most of us never see except in the

moment of death. The knockdown offered what author Derek Lundy once called "a kind of reconnaissance close to the dark country," a place where one sees the hereafter without entering into it. Should a safety harness fail or cold, tired hands not grip tightly enough as tons of water swept by, there would be no hope of survival. Peter Farlinger spelled it out clearly to everyone on deck: "If you fall off, we will search for you forever, but we will never find you."

The knockdown had proved that as skilled as the crew was, the ocean was stronger and indifferent. Each of them was being tested to the limit of their emotional and psychological capacity, and it was important for Chuck Bentley, as he looked around now, to take stock of it all dispassionately. If he guessed wrong, the next hours would be their last. He looked around at the huddled, frightened faces and asked, "What do you think? Should we go on?" The conversation wasn't long and ended with a majority decision to continue.

"We could see other boats had come around the Fastnet," Chris Punter says. "We said, 'Hey look, we're okay. We haven't lost anybody. We're reasonably under control. Let's keep going.'"

From then until dawn, Peter Farlinger and Chuck Bentley alternated steering in half-hour shifts, between times staggering below and collapsing. The four miles to Fastnet took four hours of scratching and clawing, zigging and zagging, first north and then south, making one mile toward their goal for every six or so miles sailed. With just a storm jib, *Magistri* wobbled and refused to keep a straight line. Bentley had never known such exhaustion and feared more than once the decision to continue was foolish, but having made it, he wasn't about to give up. The best way out now was through. At one point, he huddled close to Farlinger, yelled over the wind, and asked what Farlinger thought would happen if either of them became too exhausted to steer.

"There was no answer because there was no one else who could drive the boat," Bentley says. "We looked at each other and realized we had to keep doing it."

Farlinger had adopted a detached mental stance that allowed him to be less fearful than he should have been. He had not entertained the idea of quitting. If something broke, it would be trouble, but he would deal with it if and when it was necessary. Until then, his eye was on the prize: rounding Fastnet and getting safely back to Plymouth.

"The worst thing that can happen is that you drown," he says with a shrug. "Well, we are all going to die. I'm not going to stay on shore because I might die at sea. It never occurred to me that there was anything to be done other than sail the boat and sail the race."

Farlinger believed that should he or Bentley become unable to steer, someone would take their place. They would do it because they had to, and as they had to, they would find the strength. Farlinger also drew comfort from the thought that other boats were in the same life-and-death struggle. He didn't know the extent of the havoc, but assumed if others were out there and surviving, *Magistri* could too. "There are a lot worse things you can do than persevere, so we persevered," he says.

Between 2:00 a.m. and dawn, Steve Tupper could not move *Pachena* closer to Fastnet. The boat was about ten miles east and downwind of *Magistri*, but Tupper didn't know exactly where he was. He could see the Fastnet light and the lights on Cape Clear Island, which gave him a rough idea, but ever since Pat Leslie had succumbed to seasickness, navigation had been a matter of guesswork. The wind continued to shift from southwest to west, and for a while the sky cleared and the moon came out. The wind dropped temporarily, but the waves remained high. As the eye of the storm passed, the wind shifted by about thirty degrees toward the north, creating even more deadly waves and the most dangerous seas of the night. The waves had been moving more or less southwest to northeast. Now the wind was overlaying that motion with waves moving from west-northwest to east-southeast. As the wave fronts collided, the sea became confused. There were holes and spikes among the waves, which were now unpredictable.

Three people on *Pachena* were dreadfully ill, but the rest were coping, though in varying degrees of discomfort. They were disheartened by the lack of forward progress, yet try as they might there wasn't anything they could do about it. Fatigue and hypothermia were setting in, their thinking was growing fuzzy and slow, and the probability of mistake and miscalculation was rising. The boat was strong, but she was groaning under the strain. "We were thinking, We've been out there a long time, we've done our damnedest, and haven't broken anything," John Simonett says. "But if we kept on going, we might."

Then they discovered that the engine wouldn't start. Now if the jib tore, they would be helpless, as there was no other sail they could safely fly. Without an engine and with the wind shifting, the boat could be driven ashore and destroyed, just as the remnants of the Spanish Armada had been in 1588.

Simonett went below to rouse John Newton and told him he thought that they should abandon the race. Newton agreed. "I was never afraid of the sea conditions," Newton says. "We put in to Cork because we were tired. We had been battering upwind for twelve to fifteen hours. We were just worn out."

In an interview with Vancouver's *North Shore News* a week later, Newton was wistful, saying the decision to quit had been

On *Pachena's* run toward Cork, Stewart Jones is sitting, Doug Race
is at the helm, and Mike Schnetlzer is eyeing the following wave.
(*John Simonett*)

agonizing as *Pachena* was so close to the Fastnet light. "I had to think
in terms of the safety of my crew," he said. "I hope it was the right
decision. And yet, we failed."

*Pachena* hadn't planned to be anywhere near Ireland, and so
there were no detailed charts of the coast on board. None of the
crew knew these waters. but someone had heard about the Kinsale
Yacht Club, about seventeen miles from Cork, on the southeast
coast. Kinsale was about sixty miles away and a straight shot, so with
some uncertainty, but expecting that conditions would improve
and they would be able to see the Head of Kinsale landmark as they
drew closer, Simonett eased off. *Pachena* surged forward like a horse
suddenly free to gallop. She straightened up, her speed increased to

six knots, the rudder responded, the sail stopped slamming, and life was suddenly a lot better. Kinsale was about ten hours away.

Mike Schnetzler remembers how quickly the motion improved. Instead of ploughing into waves head-on every twenty seconds, the waves came once every two minutes and the boat was surfing them, taking them on an angle. *Pachena* was far easier to control and while steering still demanded full concentration, it was more manageable than it had been during the dark hours of the night.

"Basically, you are getting one-fifth to one-tenth the knocking around, once you start going downwind, so the ride and motion is ten times easier on you," Schnetzler says. The psychological lift of knowing they were out of harm's way was huge. Sunrise revealed just how big the waves they had been battling were. "It was unnerving," says Schnetzler. "We thought, Geez, we've been struggling with this all night? Are we crazy?"

Simonett still thinks about how different things might have been if they had been able to make those ten miles to Fastnet. It would have been a downwind romp to Plymouth, a cakewalk after what they'd been through. "We would have had no difficulty in finishing," he says. "Ted Turner won, but what it amounted to was Ted Turner got around Fastnet before the bulk of the storm hit."

With the boat headed to safety, Tupper and Simonett went below to rest and Doug Race took the helm. A little after dawn, Stewart Jones went below to make tea, the first hot drink since the previous afternoon. Luckily, the water hadn't boiled, because when the boat launched off a wave and then came to a dead stop, the pot and water went flying, barely missing Jones's face. He flew across the cabin as tons of water roared over the deck and squirted through the hatches. Water was spraying horizontally across the ceiling as if somebody had stuck their thumb over a faucet. "I wondered if there was anyone left on deck," Jones says.

Simonett scrambled up to find Race knee deep in water but still holding on to the wheel. Schnetzler was clinging to a backstay with both hands, one foot on the cockpit coaming and the other outside the boat. The boat had broached, the mast had skimmed the water, ripping the wind instruments out, and for a few seconds as *Pachena* skidded down the waves, her keel was out of the water.

Race had steered down the front of a wave at high speed, so fast he thought he was going to plough straight into the wave ahead of them. To avoid that collision, he turned the wheel to his left, hoping to take the oncoming wave at an angle and slide across it. But at that speed, the slight movement of the wheel had wrenched the rudder, and *Pachena* overcompensated. She climbed the wave, was banged sideways, and broached.

"It was a funny little sea that came along the crest of the wave, and away we went," Race says.

The rounding of Fastnet was a magical moment for the crew on *Magistri*. As much as they were afraid, they were elated by their achievement. As the great light at the top of the lighthouse flashed its piercing beam, they quietly celebrated attaining the pinnacle of the premier event in their ocean-racing world. They had made it. This was why for years they had made themselves available four days a week and most weekends, sweating it out in Great Lakes races. They had learned during their winter races in Florida, done on a shoestring budget and in an old boat, that they could keep up with the big boys and their deep pockets, that even though they didn't have the best or the newest this was no excuse to fail.

Chuck Bentley's relentless badgering, cajoling, and persuading, occasionally chiding them, had resulted in their doing things they had no business doing, in a boat that should not have been a winner. This was why they were able to round Fastnet in the dark, without the proper sails, in mountainous waves, lashed by hurricane-force winds whose foamy tendrils stung like a whip. Their small fibreglass craft, built by rich men to achieve a brief moment of sailing glory and then discarded, had a ringside seat as nature roared with a fury they had never seen before and would never see again.

Roger Vaughan, a journalist crewing on *Kialoa*, captured this exhilaration in an article he wrote for the *New York Times* a few weeks after the race. Vaughan later also wrote a book about his experience aboard the aluminum super-yacht, which was second to cross the finish line. *Kialoa* was almost twice as long as *Magistri*, with a mast that rose a hundred feet above the deck. Her largest foresails weighed one hundred and fifty pounds. She was strong, seaworthy, and had two hundred thousand miles under her keel at the time of the race. From the very beginning, Vaughan felt the storm was different; the night did not have the normal claustrophobic feel of such events. At the height of it, as others did, he saw that the sky was filled with stars and a high moon masked scudding clouds. The moonbeams, he wrote, peeked through the clouds and turned small patches of ocean to pure pounded silver.

"*Kialoa*'s fine racing bow sliced into the seas, carving off hunks of ocean that were splattered to either side, as foam was heaved high into the air and blown into the sails," Vaughan wrote. "The water was thick with gobs of phosphorescence that would stick on the mainsail and glow for a moment, or speed off on the wind like sparks from spent fireworks."

Vaughan's sense of wonder is not uncommon among people who engage in dangerous pursuits. They often feel fear, exhilaration, and a sense of communion with the elements, often when their lives are most at risk. In his examination of the motives and personalities of single-handed sailors, author Richard Henderson found that *being there*, whether *there* is halfway up K2 or alone in an ocean storm, imbues a sense of self-significance and self-worth, a sense of finding one's place in the world and belonging. Many sailors feel uniquely suited to what they do, so sailing in good weather and bad is an expression of themselves. Peter Farlinger was thirty-five when he took up sailing. A friend took him out for a sail, and that was that. "I didn't know how to do it, but I did, if you know what I mean," he says.

Chuck Bentley gave up teaching to take up yachting as an occupation. "I was confident from the first time I sailed," he says. "I knew it was something I could do and do very well. I felt comfortable. I think I'm a reincarnation of someone who sailed before."

Nick DeGrazia learned to sail on small boats in Chicago and has never been far from the water. "I love the peacefulness and the sound of water rushing by the hull," he says. "There's a feeling of freedom and always a bit of a thrill. There's something very exhilarating and challenging about sailing." Of the 1979 Fastnet, he says, "It was a highlight of my life." DeGrazia, like many ocean-racing sailors, relishes the physical and mental challenges that competition offers. Bad weather makes boats go fast and going fast makes the competitive juice flow. As the proverb goes, "Smooth seas do not make skillful sailors."

Some people enjoy danger because it makes them feel more alive, especially when they have survived. The adrenalin rush feels good, so they try to recreate it. Thrill-seekers aren't crazy or unbalanced, they just need action to feel good.

Maria Coffey, author of *Where the Mountain Casts Its Shadow* about her relationship with mountain climber Joe Tasker, who died during a fall from Everest, has explored the dark side of extreme adventure. She argues that in the West we are insulated from the physical dangers faced by our ancestors. Some people miss it and seek it out. For the hard core, risk is necessary, danger is part of the deal. As Sir Robin Knox-Johnston said when asked about the risks of sailing alone in the Southern Ocean, "If it was entirely safe, why would you want to go?"

There are moments on such trips when the adventurers transcend their fear and feel content and fulfilled, an awareness one mountain climber described to Maria Coffey "as a sense of intimacy with the infinite." This sensation is described in Zen Buddhism as *kensho*, a moment of feeling at one with the universe. The same thing in the Judeo-Christian tradition is often used to denote an epiphany when God is made manifest. At such a moment, one does everything right without knowing it, without effort. One's entire attention is focused on a clear goal and doing it is suddenly effortless. The depth of concentration is so intense that everything else in life falls away; one is unaware of the passage of time, one moves beyond normal consciousness into a short-lived state of flow, in modern sporting parlance, the zone. It is a sense of being intensely alive.

Bernard Moitessier often wrote about feeling at one with God, nature, and the sea when aboard his thirty-six-foot *Joshua*. After he rounded Cape Horn, he sent a message to his publisher – by slingshot to a passing ship – to say: "I am continuing non-stop towards the Pacific Islands because I am happy at sea, and perhaps also to save my soul."

As *Magistri* drew nearer to the Fastnet rock, the crew were more interested in saving their lives than their souls. Their lives hung on an invisible thread as Moitessier's had when he rounded Cape

Horn. They struggled forward in humility, knowing their survival in some measure came down to luck and because the sea allowed them to pass.

Arch Alyea did not give more than a passing consideration to his mortality, but was taken by the sense of being there. "The Fastnet wasn't some adventure that just happened," he says. "It was something you had thought about in the back of your mind for years."

He went below for his camera and managed to take a few photos. In the grainy, rain-splattered frames, you can see the lighthouse over one shoulder, men sitting with their chins tucked in, heads bowed as though in prayer, wondering, one thinks, whether they will live to see the sun come up.

Nick DeGrazia dragged himself on deck and each tremor by the boat made him wonder whether that little thing, whatever it was, was about to break. It seemed to take hours for the lighthouse to draw abeam. "I don't now how many times we tacked to get around that damn rock, but it was many," he says. "It took forever."

John Hollidge was cheerful and reassuring, reminding the crew they still had choices and should they decide to quit, they could. "People get frightened if they feel they don't have an option," he says. "People stay more confident if they know they do." Andre Calla had been unable to remain in the cabin since the knockdown. He was like a nervous cat, jumpy, on high alert and eager for something to do. The race had taken on a dreamlike feel to Peter Milligan. Lying below in the dark, feeling every quiver and creak, his nerves were scraped raw. He was still listening to the radio, hearing distress calls, some quite matter of fact, others pleading for assistance. "You're hearing people who are probably going down, and you try to imagine what it would be like if you were taking on water or pitch-poling," he says. "These were people you were never going to see again. It was very scary, very frightening."

Fastnet lighthouse on a
calm day. (*Rolex Fastnet*)

At Fastnet, he came up on deck and saw the flashing light, green
water rising in slow motion and smashing against the lighthouse,
the spray seeming to fly to the full 125-foot height of the structure.
He could feel the boat being sucked back and forth by the huge
swell breaking on the rocks, a terrifying sensation of being dragged
toward certain death. "You really felt at the mercy of it all," he says.

As a pink glow began to paint the grey sky, the lighthouse
became more visible, perched on the rock like a stovepipe. The
wind had shifted to the west and so to get past the rock, *Magistri*
beat south toward the rock, then north toward the Irish coast. Only
four and a half miles separates the Fastnet Light from Cape Clear

Island, the most southerly point in the Irish Republic. Chuck Bentley remembers John Hollidge pointing to a dark shape with a light flashing. It was the lighthouse on Cape Clear, but Bentley did not know what it was. Hollidge shouted across the din, but could not be clearly heard. "I thought he said Cape Fear," Bentley says. "I thought to myself, Man, that's well named."

Fastnet Rock is also known as the Teardrop of Ireland, because it is the last sight many emigrants saw of their homeland. The first lighthouse there was moved from Cape Clear in 1854 and the tower that exists now went into service in 1904. It is the tallest and widest rock lighthouse tower in the British Isles. It took five years to build, and each Cornish granite stone is hand-carved and weighs between one and three-quarter and three tons.

As they drew near Fastnet, Peter Farlinger took over the helm. He wanted to give the rock a wide berth, fearing that if he turned too soon he would be driven back onto the rocks. Worried by just that eventuality, Chris Punter had earlier persuaded Bentley to turn on the engine. It was left in neutral, offering psychological comfort, if not much else. In those seas it would have been useless.

The storm took every ounce of Farlinger's strength, and he learned the only way to get enough leverage to move the tiller was to crouch in the cockpit, his backside against the combing, pushing with his feet. Inch by inch he gained on the lighthouse, beating up and down, first toward and then away, until finally they were past the rock and it was well to the stern. With a final effort, he tacked, and *Magistri* started to run with the storm toward Plymouth.

"It is that moment at Fastnet Rock itself, with everything in the balance, that I think of most," Farlinger later wrote. "Every few seconds I'd look to leeward, checking to see if we were really making progress. I'd see those enormous waves crashing over the rocks, pounding almost right up to the lighthouse, and I'd think, We are not going to go there. We will not stop now. Whatever it takes, we'll do it.

"And then, in some strange way, I'd think how absolutely, incredibly beautiful the scene around us was – a truly classic seascape of wind, spray, and great cresting waves. And of that lonely lighthouse looking like a Stonehenge. Just simply beautiful. And I'd wonder, How did we ever manage to get ourselves here?"

Punter was also aware of the majesty of the moment, and it was only later that he considered what might have happened. "To discount luck and say we did that through sheer seamanship is probably folly. Yeah, luck played a huge part in it."

On board *Kialoa*, Roger Vaughan had earlier had much the same reaction. He knew the spectacle was unlike any he was likely to see again. "Beauty of the sort that amounts to religious experience must rank high on my personal list," he wrote. "I am not a churchgoer. But always at sea, my agnosticism falters. For at sea is when the concept of cosmic unity is most difficult to deny."

*Magistri* came so close to the lighthouse during the turn that Nick DeGrazia and Andre Calla were convinced they could see the lighthouse keeper wearing a white fisherman's sweater, coffee cup in hand, watching the madmen pass by. Once they were around the lighthouse, it receded quickly, at last blinking from behind the boat.

# 14

# Dawn, Tuesday

**"The best form of tenacity I know is expressed in a
Danish fur trapper's principle: The next mile is the only
one a person really has to make."**

– BROADCASTER ERIC SEVAREID

~~~~~~~~~~~~~~~~~~~~~~

ABOUT ONE HUNDRED miles to the southeast of *Magistri*, as
the skies started to lighten on Tuesday morning, *Magic* was drifting.
The storm's force had peaked two hours earlier, at about 2:00 a.m.,
with gusts between sixty and eighty knots. The waves were as tall
as a four-storey building. Fear doesn't adequately describe the
feeling as the crew sat below in their wooden cocoon, braced for
the next blow. As often as not the boat was forced onto her side,
knocked down like a pin in a bowling alley, and the crew fell in an
ungainly heap on the opposite bunk. On the way over, those who
caught a glimpse out the window saw nothing but water. Then the
boat popped up as its buoyant force took over.

A few times, *Magic* was knocked over so far that her mast
touched the water, and the crew could see the boat fall down to the
bottom of the wave, come upright, and carry on up the next wave.

At the top, the wind smashed into the hull; the boat shuddered and rolled down the backside. It tested one's sanity.

The crew often ended up with their feet on the cabin roof as *Magic* was rolled to almost horizontal. They got used to the motion, or at least became numbed to it. There was nothing that could be done. Occasionally, they opened the hatch only to see that spray and spume had turned their world completely grey.

Other boats of *Magic's* size were also being battered, rolling over through 360 degrees, some losing masts, others seeing their windows implode, their cabin tops peeled off. Some were going end over end – as they vainly tried to run before the storm. For some reason, *Magic* didn't face the ultimate test, although without her rudder, she was more vulnerable than any other boat her size and in the worst quadrant of the storm. The sounds were ominous, and in the darkness, their muscles and minds clenched, the crew could only wait for the next jolt, and the waiting was dreadful, knowing that a big one was coming, but not when. And when it arrived, Peter Hoosen-Owen says, "It was like the side of a house breaking over us."

A steady trickle of water dripped through the hatch boards in the companionway. The boat was in constant motion, flexing at the joints, and the hatch boards were ill-fitting as a result of the contortions. The crack in the supporting wooden strut that had given way grew bigger with each lurch, but did not entirely break. The six holes in the stern where the rudder had been ripped away luckily stayed above the waterline. Even so, water splashed in, and the crew took turns bailing with a bucket and pouring the water down the sink. It gave them something to do. An emergency light gave some illumination, but by morning the batteries were almost dead and they turned off the light.

Courage, they say, is acting in spite of fear, and somehow these ordinary men managed their fear in an extraordinary way. They did not panic, they did not give in to despair, and they continued to believe in one another and their ability to survive.

"There are things that you just hold in to yourself, little things," Hoosen-Owen says. "It was bad, we knew that, so you tell yourself it's a question of waiting until daylight and then you can see what you're up against, because until daylight there was nothing to be done."

Peter Whipp adds, "I have to say it concentrated the mind a lot."

After Doug Race's misjudgment running down the back of a wave, *Pachena's* sixty-mile run to Crosshaven became progressively easier, if only in comparison to the earlier conditions. In the shelter of the southern coast of Ireland, the waves were less severe, though the wind was still blowing in the fifties. The difference was that as *Pachena* reached across the waves, she rode up and down more comfortably and the feeling of being a crash-test dummy disappeared. With Steve Tupper and John Simonett below, the others were left in charge.

At about noon, *Pachena* passed the Old Head of Kinsale, and a short while later found the entrance to Cork Harbour. They radioed ahead, and a boat from the Royal Cork Yacht Club came out and towed them into a slip in Crosshaven, on the west side of Cork Harbour. Many boats were still unreported at that point, including all three of the Irish team, two of which had lost their rudders. Stewart Jones felt a sense of unease as they were towed alongside the clubhouse and tied off at the quay. "There were boats with no masts, boats with no stanchions and lifelines, and a boat with no mast, no people and half full of water," he says. "That's a godawful eerie feeling to walk along a dock and see that."

John Simonett and Steve Tupper had long since had a feeling that the storm had taken a toll, but had shunted the thought into the background. As they tied up, Simonett said something inane to the elderly club member helping them in, something about "quite a storm out there." The man looked at him, nodded, and said, "Yes, it was. There has been heavy loss of life." A heavy loss of life? thought Simonett.

Tupper made a beeline for the telephone and called his wife in Vancouver. He told her that, no matter who called or what they said, everyone on *Pachena* was okay. He asked that she spread the word. It was a timely call. A half an hour later, a friend phoned her to say *Pachena* had been reported missing.

By the end of the day, forty-five Fastnet boats in various states were anchored at Crosshaven and Kinsale. The *Cork Examiner* interviewed the crew of *Livewire*, a yacht from Dun Laoghaire, a few miles from Dublin. *Livewire* had withdrawn from the race when its electrical systems failed. Many of her crew were already bravely talking about the next Fastnet, but Michael Buckley was not among them. "I'm thinking of taking up golf or something similar," he said. "It at least allows you to walk off the course when the going gets rough."

As *Magistri* began her return trip, she was still two hundred miles from Plymouth. Fatigue had robbed the crew of much more than a semblance of energy, and most of them now slept where they fell. But for Chuck Bentley and Peter Farlinger, there was no rest. They alternated steering for about fifteen minutes at a time. Somehow they also managed to act as deck hands and cheerleaders for the crew that stayed awake. After the rounding, Peter Cowern kept Bentley

After Magistri rounded Fastnet, Arch Alyea took this shot over
*Magistri's* starboard side, looking back toward the lighthouse.
(*Arch Alyea*)

company, adding his upper-body strength to help move the tiller. He
found the storm even more frightening now that he could see the
height of the waves. The wind had eased slightly through the earlier
hours of the morning, but it was still singing through the rigging.
Cowern was afraid, but he was also enthralled by the force of the
boat's acceleration as it surfed down the waves, by the snap and snarl
of the wind. He felt privileged to be witnessing a rare spectacle and,
at the same time, puny in the face of this relentless and indefatiga-
ble opponent. Even though the sun was climbing higher, they would
lose sight of it as *Magistri* slid down into the troughs, then it would
blind them as they climbed to the top of the next wave. At one point,
Cowern looked over his shoulder. "There was a wave, horrendous,
huge," he says. "I imagine it was forty, fifty feet and it was breaking
right over the top of us. We were completely under water, buried,

holding on for our lives. Then the boat shook and shuddered and the water disappeared and we continued on. It was just unbelievable." Cowern says. "It was amazing, completely exhilarating."

Even though the motion had eased, the noise was still considerable and the vibrations below were cacophonous. Fred Goode felt it was time to go up for air. "It can get pretty bad in the Gulf Stream when you're going against the current, but I had never been on a boat that shook like that," he says. "The waves were breaking from behind and it would shake, shake, and shake. I remember thinking, I hope she's well made because she's taking a shit-kicking."

Chuck Bentley had a sixth sense that allowed him to thread his way through the waves with precision and certainty. All over the course in these early hours, boat-breaking waves were hurling sailors from their boats, but *Magistri* was untouched, running before nature's roar with a triple-reefed mainsail and boom eased way out, smoking down the waves at eight knots and more. Often, as she charged over a wave, the front half of the boat floated in midair until the weight of the boat pulled it down. Bentley was astonished when sea birds skimming the waves flew under the boat. The implication that there was nothing underneath him except thirty feet of air was hard to believe. Holding firmly on to the tiller, he leaned forward for a closer look to reassure himself he wasn't hallucinating. "It was an incredible sensation," he says.

The dirty grey sky gave way to streaks of blue and some pink as the clouds started to break up. Like Cowern, Chris Punter was shaken by the size of the waves and amazed that they had survived the night. As he stared at the enormous walls of water that towered over him, then melted away under the boat, he was overwhelmed by a sense of the divine. Punter is not a religious man, but when the clouds parted and a ray of sunshine bathed the top of the wave, he felt certain it was a beacon, illuminating the way home, and that they would survive. "I had to believe God was saying, 'Here's the sun, here's the light, come on through this big cathedral, I'm opening up for you,'" Punter says.

Arch Alyea, focused on his task, wanted to raise more sail, but nobody had the stomach for it. The mainsail had ripped at the cringles when someone had tried to flatten it while it was still reefed and tied to the boom. So *Magistri* ambled along, and gradually life returned. The crew roused themselves and came on deck, happy to feel the sun on their face, smell the wind, and see for themselves what they had endured.

All of a sudden everyone realized just how hungry they were. Whatever food could be found was tossed into the cockpit – sweet rolls, crackers, hunks of cheese, bread, water, soft drinks. Everyone gorged and couldn't believe how good such simple things tasted. After they'd eaten, Andre Calla and Arch Alyea stitched the torn mainsail, and with one reef out they become braver. They hoisted a small jib, held out by a spinnaker pole. Running more or less downwind, wing on wing, *Magistri*'s speed now was nine or ten knots.

The crew shook off the last of its lethargy when a French Admiral's Cup boat called *Revolootion* blasted by, flying a small spinnaker. They first saw it as a red dot on the horizon, but very quickly she was alongside, then past. It was an odd little thirty-footer with a lilac "loo" strapped to its stern rail. Emboldened by this, Alyea hoisted a small, heavy spinnaker, known as the chicken chute, and *Magistri* got back in business. Says Nick DeGrazia, "When we saw him draw alongside with the boom poled out, rocking back and forth, but under control, we said to each other, 'Come on, what are we? Chopped liver?'"

*Magic's* rescue came midmorning, as *Pachena* was tying up in Cork. A little after 9:30 a.m. Tuesday, the crew heard the drone of an aircraft engine. Whipp eased back the hatch, but at first couldn't see anything, although he managed to raise the RAF Nimrod on the radio. The pilot couldn't see them, but Whipp could now see the plane. The pilot rolled to the left and then the right and asked Whipp to respond if he could see the motion. Whipp confirmed the sighting, and the Nimrod relayed the co-ordinates to the air rescue centre at Culdrose. The pilot told *Magic* to hang on; help was on the way.

About twenty minutes later, they heard the sound of helicopter blades. Whipp still hadn't decided to abandon ship, because tough as things were, the boat was more or less sound, the crew was safe, and the storm was sure to abate sooner or later. He found it hard to give up. "Maybe we were being a bit brave, but we told the pilot, 'Look, there are people out here in far worse shape. Leave us and get them,'" Whipp said.

The pilot was in no mood to negotiate. He impatiently told Whipp that he was running out of fuel, and it was now or never. "If you don't get in now, that's it. We're not going to come looking for you," he said. Whipp took a hard look at his two mates, thought about the two in the berths, and, as Hoosen-Owen recalls, said, "'Oh blow it, let's go.'"

The pilot asked *Magic* to set off an orange flare and then another, as markers. The evacuation was carried out in an orderly sequence laid down by the pilot. The crew jumped, or were pushed, into the water, wearing foul-weather gear and life jackets, but no sea boots. When they had drifted a safe distance away from the boat, a diver attached to a fifty-foot cable was lowered into the water. Wearing oversized flippers, he moved powerfully through the water to the bobbing sailor. He put the sling over the man's head and shoulders and under each arm, clasped him in bear hug, and locked his legs around his waist. The diver raised his arm as a signal to hoist.

As Hoosen-Owen rose above the waves toward the helicopter, he realized why the boat had been so difficult to spot. "I couldn't see anything," he says. "Nothing at all. It looked like milk. White, just white as far as the eye could see."

Whipp was the last to go and after one last look, he jumped off the *Magic*. The diver couldn't get the sling over his shoulder and Whipp fell back into the water. As he thrashed in the waves, Whipp was horrified to see the diver hauled up and the helicopter fly off and out of sight. *Magic* was a few hundred feet upwind, but he knew he couldn't get to her. His thoughts were interrupted by the sound of the helicopter returning. The diver was lowered once more and this time fit the sling securely around him. The pilot had been unable to keep the craft level and, worried about crashing, had gone around for another pass. Such were the small and large acts of heroism that day.

The Wessex turned and headed for the Cornish coast and *Magic* disappeared behind a wave. It was the last the crew ever saw of her. As their rescuers related the extent of the Fastnet disaster, Whipp and his friends thought about luck and the odds that *Magic*'s flares would have been seen by *Evergreen*. They wondered if the Canadians had survived.

A French trawler found *Magic* adrift, took her in tow, and, as was her captain's right under international law, stripped her of all her valuables – winches, electronics, hardware, fixtures. The trawler then passed her to a Royal Navy tug, and while being towed to port *Magic* sank. Whipp believes it was an act of mercy.

"I think the Navy took one look at her and said, 'The owner

will thank us for this,' and opened up the engine. I'm only guessing, because that wasn't the official line."

The sun was rising over the Irish Sea, but aboard *Evergreen*, the crew was almost too tired to welcome the change in weather. As the boat moved away from the storm, the wind eased. The seas were still enormous, but the wave tops were no longer breaking, and it was much easier to steer. But as on *Magistri*, long after it was safe to raise more sail, they were still running with only a storm jib and a small piece of mainsail. Steve Killing was at the helm midmorning and remembers thinking they should do something, but no one had any energy left. "We were so tired," he says. "*Evergreen* was creeping along, inching along, and nobody wants to put anything up. Finally when we're getting closer to land, we shake out a reef."

By 10:00 a.m. they were past the Scilly Isles and heading into the English Channel. The sun was getting stronger, and every degree rise in temperature lifted their spirits. The sight of land made a huge difference. "It became sort of fun," Green says. *Evergreen* was surfing in thirty knots of winds with about seventy miles to go to Plymouth. It seemed now that all it would take was prudent seamanship and concentration to make it home. Spirits were so high that there were now jokes, where twelve hours earlier there had been prayers. "We had no idea what was going on out there, still had no clue," Ron Barr says. "We just knew we had been through a storm that none of us had ever seen before, and we had got through it in a boat that had no right to be there."

Dennis Aggus took over at the helm and tied his safety line to a stanchion. He knew it was a dumb idea, but felt awkward using the jackline, which was constantly getting twisted and hampering his movement. "It was foolish, because if I had gone over, the stanchion would have ripped out, and if the boat had rolled I would have been trapped underneath," he says.

Nobody had eaten much for twenty-four hours, and so Don Green asked Aggus to put something together. The best he could do was what they called a Lake Huron breakfast, something they had eaten the previous summer when they had been dismasted during the Canada's Cup. It was pecan pie and orange juice. Aggus had squirrelled the pies away, and amazingly they were more or less intact.

As the day wore on, the wind and the waves dropped. By the time *Evergreen* approached Plymouth in the late afternoon, the conditions were ideal so they hoisted a spinnaker. It was a lovely sailing day, not a cloud in the sky. They checked the boat for wear and tear and found that not a thing had broken, not a line, not a turnbuckle, not a shackle. Nothing.

At about 6:00 p.m., *Evergreen* coasted into Plymouth Sound. The crew had mixed emotions as the end of their journey grew near. They had come to England as champions and were leaving not as winners but as survivors. The competition, the weather, the boats, all of it had been underestimated. Amid these private thoughts, Don Green was puzzled when a small powerboat came buzzing out of Queen Anne's Battery in Millbay Dock, saw them, and went racing back. As *Evergreen* followed the boat in, Green saw that hundreds of people had gathered there. The crowd hushed as the boat came close, then erupted into a spontaneous round of applause. "We wondered why they were there," Green said. "Why are they clapping? What's going on?"

There wasn't much room in the basin so they tied *Evergreen* to another boat. The crew made half-hearted attempts to clean up, and

Steve Killing was tending to some lines when his eye caught a rapid movement in the crowd. His wife, Margaret, came bounding across the rafted boats, followed by Ron Barr's wife, Pat. There were hugs and tears, whispered words, and loving embraces. It was then they learned about the sinkings, deaths, and rescues that were now all over the news media. Among the many rumours those on shore had heard was that *Evergreen* was missing. This only confirmed the prevailing wisdom that if any boat was sure to go down, it was her. Someone made that comment on the dock in the presence of the Canadian wives and girlfriends. "I thought it was a pretty goofy thing to say," Killing says.

In the midst of the celebrations, a man who looked like a naval officer, but could have been a steward at the yacht club, arrived with a tray and a bottle of whisky. Then a couple of haggard-looking guys in brand-new white running shoes marched on board. The glasses were offered around and the whisky poured. Nobody knew who the two men were, and Ron Barr, as thankful as he was for the whisky, was annoyed that strangers had wandered on board uninvited. When one of them said he was from a boat called *Magic*, that cleared the air, another round was poured, things warmed up, and pretty soon there was a party going on. "They figured we saved their lives," Barr says.

*Magic's* crew was among seventy-five rescued sailors who ended up at the air naval station at Culdrose in Cornwall before the day was done. The flight took less than half an hour, and once off the helicopter they had shed their wet clothes, hopped into hot baths, and were offered a tumbler of brandy to warm themselves up. The bottle of brandy ran dry before it reached Hoosen-Owen, so he ended up with Bushmill's Irish Whiskey from somebody's private store. It was his first introduction to Irish whiskey, a taste he still savours. The bath and the alcohol combined with fatigue to knock

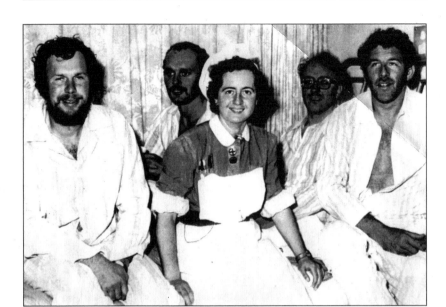

Peter Whipp (left), Peter Hoosen-Owen (right), and two others
from *Magic*'s crew pose with a nurse at the Royal Navy's infirmary
at Culdrose, Cornwall. Soon after the photograph was taken, they left
the base for Plymouth. (*Royal Navy*)

them out, and when they awoke some hours later their clothes were
clean and they had new Royal Naval–issue running shoes.

With so many rescues, their beds were needed for the incoming, so an air force driver was rounded up and the *Magic* crew was
driven to Plymouth. They arrived by about 5:00 p.m., managed to
get a hotel for a night, and then went down to the harbour to find
out what was going on.

By then only two boats had finished the race. *Condor of Bermuda*
crossed the line first at 1:55 p.m., followed by *Kialoa* just under half
an hour later. *Mistress Quickly*, another Bermudian boat, was the
third to finish at about 6:30 p.m.

Margaret Killing and Pat Barr had cut short their tour of Cornwall to return to Plymouth. That Tuesday afternoon they hung around the Royal Western Yacht Club, hoping for news and waiting for the updated list of boats sunk, missing, and reported safe to be posted. Rita Fitzpatrick and Sandra Green, who were also in Cornwall, were unaware of the extent of the storm's damage until later that day. They spent Tuesday sightseeing and wandering around the Cornish village of Looe, twenty miles west of Plymouth. Monday night had been extremely windy, but they didn't watch any television until the five o'clock BBC news on Tuesday.

"We were just beside ourselves," Sandy Green says. "It was one of these surreal kind of experiences. The RAF rescuers were pulling people off sinking boats, and you're watching all this and looking for familiar faces on the TV. You're holding on and hoping for the best, but thinking about *what if.*"

In Plymouth, the worried wives waiting at the Royal Western Yacht Club couldn't find *Evergreen* on any list, either as continuing to race or having abandoned it. Margaret Killing and Pat Barr were wondering what to do when they caught Peter Whipp's eye. Whipp was at the yacht club getting an update when he noticed their team shirts and introduced himself. When he told them the story of the previous night, the women knew that until midnight at least, *Evergreen* had been safe. It was not long after he met them that *Evergreen* pulled in to the harbour.

When the race started, John Bobyk and his wife, Ann, had gone to Maidstone in Kent, where John's company had an office. They spent the night in London and came back to Plymouth on an afternoon train. While John retrieved their bags, Ann went to a newsstand for an afternoon paper. Then Bobyk heard her scream.

"I thought somebody had done something to her," he says. "I ran over and she was holding a newspaper and her hand was shaking like crazy. It was a picture of *Evergreen* with a banner headline that said, 'Disaster at Sea.' We had a feeling of absolute dread. You didn't know what to say or do and couldn't help but think the worst."

The Bobyks made all haste down to the Royal Western Yacht Club just as *Evergreen* pulled in.

"The guys looked terrible, very quiet, very subdued," Bobyk says. "They looked battered and worn out. I'll always remember the bloodshot eyes and Don, just so grateful he had brought everyone back alive."

Some of the crew were hustled away by their wives and those that remained wandered over to the clubhouse. When the dishevelled group bellied up to the bar, somebody asked what boat they were from. When they said *Evergreen*, a cheer went up and a round of drinks appeared.

Don Green placed a call to the Looe Hotel, and Sandy and Rita drove to Plymouth. At the yacht club bar, Sandy recalls seeing "this wet group of guys, bedraggled, bearded and looking a mess." After a quick reunion, the Greens and Fitzpatricks drove back to Looe for the night, a trip Sandy Green recalls as almost completely silent with the men lost in thought.

Al Megarry can't remember when he left the bar. He was swapping stories and reliving the dramatic moments, the hard edges of memory blunted by alcohol. At some point, he figured he should call home. His uncle, Roy Megarry, publisher of Toronto's *Globe & Mail* newspaper, had taken a special interest in the race. The wire services had initially reported *Evergreen* as possibly lost, having mistaken the race committee's status of not having reported in with having sunk. The story was pretty confused for the Wednesday newspapers, which were about to go to press as Megarry made his late-night call. The papers were relying on early reports that had unreliable numbers of boats abandoned and crew drowned. In his article, the *Hamilton Spectator*'s Stewart Brown, who was in Plymouth, chose his words carefully. "Evergreen has not reported her location since Sunday afternoon," he wrote in a front-page story that appeared on Tuesday. "Radio failure is suspected to be the reason."

*Evergreen* had reported in on Monday night to say she was abandoning the race, but the message had not been passed on, one of many that fell by the wayside. The race committee was spectacularly ill-equipped to cope with a disaster on this scale, having no precedent, no public relations machinery, and no war room to coordinate the flow of information. News, such as it was, came from calls from individual boats to relatives or friends in Plymouth, who relayed the information in bits and pieces. Rumours, mistakes, wishful thinking, all made it into reports.

The popular press had its hands full evaluating a story that had until then largely been confined to the sports pages. In many cases, the stories lacked context because editors didn't know how the sport worked, how the race was run, and the responsibilities assumed by those who entered the event. The story was deemed newsworthy only once ships were being abandoned, air and sea rescues were mounted, and people were dying. It was dramatic stuff. For radio and TV reporters, there wasn't much time for reflection and they were quick to judge: The boats were too small and unsafe, the fleet too inexperienced, the race committee at fault for starting the race, the rescue too little, too late. That 20-20 hindsight was coupled with mistakes in reporting who was lost, how many people had been rescued, and who had died. Unfortunately, in many cases "not-reported-in" became a euphemism for having gone down.

Roy Megarry called his brother George to tell him what was going on in the Irish Sea. None of this was relayed to Al's mother, Gloria. Instead, George hid the morning paper and did everything he could to see she remained uninformed until things became clear.

It all fell apart when Gloria took a call from a friend to say she was so sorry to hear about her loss. Gloria didn't know what to think, but was beside herself with worry when she accepted a collect call from a drunk in a bar in Plymouth, England.

"I said, 'Hi Mom,'" Megarry says. "She said, 'Allan?' Then I heard her crying. I'm drunk as a newt, but all of a sudden everyone's happy."

George took the phone, and as he later told the *Hamilton Spectator*, "I asked him if he was scared. He said, 'No. I was terrified.'"

Ron Barr's parents thought he was dead until he called. A *Hamilton Spectator* photographer showed up at Jim Talmage's front door and asked his fretting wife, Greta, to pose with a picture of Jim. She was pretty angry, but agreed to let a picture be taken of her picking up the telephone receiver. The newspaper was helpful in keeping her abreast of the news via Stewart Brown in Plymouth. Greta ended up on Barbara Frum's CBC Radio show *As It Happens*. She was at the Royal Hamilton Yacht Club in the midst of the crisis and picked up the phone to find Frum on the line. She filled in a national audience with the latest developments.

At the Green family home, nineteen-year-old Sharon and her fiancé, Tim Stearn, were watching the news and answering the phone. "I was in Toronto when I heard about the storm and I nearly had heart failure," she told the *Toronto Star* in an interview. Her worst moment was when one local radio station called and as soon as she answered she heard a telltale click to say she was live. Stearn made the point in the interview that no amount of preparation would have been enough for conditions like that. "No yacht race I can think of in modern history has had that big of a problem with storms," he said. "Even experienced seaman will sail for years and not run into conditions like that." Sharon's anxiety turned to relief when her parents called from Looe to tell her that everyone was safe.

In Ireland, at yacht designer Ron Holland's farm, not far from Cork, Stewart Jones also found himself at the other end of Barbara Frum's phone. Holland had returned to Cork after being airlifted from *Golden Apple*. Doug Race had sailed across the Atlantic with Holland and they had become friends. Now Holland offered Race and Jones a place to stay. When Frum tracked Holland down, intending to talk to him about broken rudders, she got the matter-of-fact Jones instead. The interview went on for fifteen minutes with Jones regaling her in detail about the trials and tribulations *Pachena* had endured. In a classic end-of-interview question, Frum asked whether he would do it again.

Without even thinking, Jones said, "Absolutely."

That evening, Ron Barr was so tightly wound he figured he would snap. He couldn't sit still, couldn't focus, and couldn't sleep. His thoughts were turned inward in a confusing jumble. He had a shower and went to the bar for a couple of drinks. It didn't help. Nor did the BBC's eight o'clock news. The announcer sombrely informed viewers that eight sailors were confirmed dead. Barr went out for dinner and was back in his room by 10:00 p.m. He tried to sleep but still couldn't. He got up, flicked on the TV, and caught the eleven o'clock news. Now there were eleven sailors dead. Dead? People don't die in sailing races. It's supposed to be challenging, yes, but deadly? The more Barr thought about the news, the more overwhelming it became. "I just couldn't believe it, and I broke down and started crying," he says.

# *15*

# *Plymouth*

"Life is a succession of lessons which
must be lived to be understood."

– HELEN KELLER

~~~~~~~~~~~~~~~~

*T*HAT EVENING, JOHN and Anne Bobyk joined Peter Whipp,
Peter Hoosen-Owen, and Tim Allison for dinner. Most of *Evergreen's*
crew had retreated to their hotels to lick their wounds and decom-
press in private. The Bobyks had been walking through the
Barbican, the trendy quayside area of Plymouth, when they were
accosted by what John Bobyk says were "three dishevelled-looking
guys in ill-fitting clothes who embraced and hugged us." The
Bobyks were wearing *Evergreen* sweaters, which was how Whipp
identified them and insisted they join him for dinner.

Over the meal, the full story of *Magic's* rescue unfolded, but
with the wine piling onto three days of fatigue, Whipp was so tired
during one lull in conversation his head fell forward and if a
restraining hand hadn't been on his shoulder he would have fallen
face first onto the table. Even so, the story tumbled out – the

rudder, the flares, *Evergreen*'s attempts to help, the radio message relayed to Condor, the helicopter rescue.

"They attributed their salvation to the fact that *Evergreen* stood by them," Bobyk says.

Peter-Hoosen Owen sank, he says, "God knows how many pints of ale" as he listened and pondered his enormous good fortune in being alive. The sheer luck of *Magic*'s survival had struck home earlier as he walked through the yacht basin looking at boats he once thought were indestructible. Many were a sorry sight: twisted metal and tangled ropes, broken booms and shattered masts. When people asked him later to describe what had happened and how he felt about it, he was often at a loss for words to express the fear, the wonder, the sense of brotherhood. He discussed this later with his wife's father, who had been in the British Merchant Navy during the Second World War. "He said, 'Now you know what I mean when I talk about the sea. These other buggers don't have a clue.'"

The dinner was marred by the victorious Ted Turner and his crew, who were celebrating their victory at a nearby table in the small restaurant. Their laughter and loud conversation filled the room. It sounded to Whipp as though they were rehearsing for a press conference, and he was struck by the lack of humility. "It made me ill to listen to it," he says.

Bobyk remembers Turner talking loudly about how the race committee had been wrong to allow small boats in the race and lamenting that all boats weren't required to have a transmitting radio, not just one that could receive. The criticism might have been valid, but Bobyk found Turner's tone and demeanour grating.

Turner knew the *Evergreen* and *Magistri* crews from the Florida winter circuit, and they had seen one another often during the various dinners and parties during the Admiral's Cup. At one dinner, at which both Turner and Don Green were guests, Turner got up mid-meal and left because he was bored, leaving Green to apologize on his behalf. At another dinner, Turner entertained the table with a litany of the flaws in *Evergreen's* design, construction, and seaworthiness, as Green sat beside him. "That was Ted's nature, very loud-mouthed, very bristly, but a great sailor," Green says charitably.

Turner's comments about *Evergreen* were the continuation of a harangue about the changing nature of ocean racing that he often voiced. The trend was away from heavy, well-built boats to lighter, stripped-down fibreglass shells. *Evergreen* was an example of what was wrong. On one occasion during the SORC races in Florida, Turner had walked past *Evergreen* and said to Green, "Oh my God, is that what we're coming to? Is this where yachting is going? I wouldn't set foot on that boat."

Jim Talmage and Alan Jeyes ended up at the Holiday Inn in Plymouth. There were no available rooms, but while Talmage and Jeyes were at the reception desk, a businessman overheard their conversation and offered to share his. They put a mattress on the floor and spent the night there. In the lobby next morning, Turner saw Talmage and, recognizing him as *Evergreen* crew from his shirt, sauntered over. "You guys still alive?" he said.

*Condor of Bermuda* broke Turner's 1971 Fastnet speed record by seven and a half hours when she crossed the finishing line at the western edge of the Plymouth breakwater Tuesday afternoon. The seventy-seven-foot yacht had taken seventy-one and a half hours to complete the course, for an average speed of 8.5 knots. Since half the race had been in very light air, it was an impressive average speed. The two-time Whitbread around-the-world sailor Rob James later said the waves were the worst he ever experienced, including those in the Southern Ocean and near the infamous Cape Horn.

*Condor* had been built for the 1977 Whitbread and in the winter of 1979 had been overhauled with an eye to winning the Fastnet. Her keel was replaced, the last thirty feet of her hull was reshaped, and her mast extended. She went to the Southern Ocean racing circuit in February 1979 with high expectations of beating *Kialoa* but came up short. So a new, even taller mast was installed, giving her 10 per cent more sail area. In this race, she had a crew of twenty-two, including nine New Zealanders who had sailed the boat around the world in the 1977 Whitbread.

Owner Bob Bell's reward for the expensive modification was to beat *Kialoa* by thirty minutes, gaining more than an hour and a half on the 251 miles from the Fastnet Rock to Plymouth. *Condor* simply flew. She was ten minutes up on *Kialoa* as they rounded the Bishop Rock lighthouse at the southwest edge of the Scilly Isles, gaining twenty more before the finish. Skipper Peter Blake later said in an interview, "We pushed this mother as no boat has ever been pushed before. We cracked on every square inch of rag we dared."

*Condor* hoisted a spinnaker after heading into the Channel, and at times her speed exceeded twenty-nine knots. She was knocked down more than once, and after one broach the boat stalled and turned its head to the wind, so that the spinnaker filled from the front, pushing the boat backwards at four or five knots. The startled helmsman spun the wheel, the boat pivoted on her keel, and with a loud crack the spinnaker filled and the boat hurtled forward again at fourteen knots.

Dennis Conner's *Williwaw* came fifteenth and he, too, was blasé about the dangers – publicly, anyway. "It's no worse than the Indianapolis 500 race," Conner told the *New York Times*. "We'll take our chances. The danger is part of it. We were racing all the time."

For all his bravado, Conner gave his wife a different impression. When a reporter called her at home in San Diego, she said, "I could tell he had been scared."

For Turner, it was gratifying that he won the race by four hours on corrected time, which took into account that *Condor* was eighteen feet longer than his boat, *Tenacious*. It added to a trophy haul that already included that year's Miami-Nassau and Miami-Montego Bay in the Florida winter circuit and capped a long stretch of victories that peaked with the 1977 America's Cup.

When Turner was asked about the worst thing that happened during the race, he echoed Dennis Conner, saying, "When I was told that some little boat was the winner, I had four hours of bitter disappointment before it was straightened out. It was a big sea all right, but we pressed on and never thought about stopping racing. There was one or two seasick, but at the height of the storm we had steak dinner."

During another dockside interview, Turner made light of the storm, saying he had had "just a wonderful ride. For thirty seconds, I wondered what would happen if it blew any harder. It didn't, and I didn't have to worry any more," he said. He later tempered his comments to tip his hat to the conditions, saying, "I will grant you, it was rough. We couldn't have taken much more wind and continued to race, but we were never in danger. If I thought we were in danger, I would have pulled out. Really, I'm amazed that more weren't lost."

Amid the hubris, there was also humour. When asked what he thought of English weather, Turner said, "Well, I didn't like it very much, but I guess you British people don't mind it, otherwise you'd all be Spanish."

Despite the loss of life, Turner maintained it was still a safe race, as long as you had a good boat. He had feared that this sort of incident might happen and wondered about the advisability of sending small boats on a 605-mile race. But he didn't let the loss of life dishearten him. "It's no use crying. The king is dead, long live the king," he said.

*Tenacious* had rounded the Rock in fifth place at about 6:30 p.m. Monday. By midnight, she was down to her smallest working jib and three reefs in her main but was still making ten knots. All night she sailed under a number-four genoa; the mainsail was fully down and lashed to the boom. At first light, the crew had set a trysail and increased their speed toward Bishop Rock, the westernmost point of the Scilly Isles.

Turner's son Teddy Jr. says that soon after first light, *Tenacious* was knocked down twice. During one knockdown, the navigator, British-born Peter Bowker, was on deck with the radio direction finder trying to get a fix on Bishop Rock. The boat broached and Bowker was knocked so hard by a wave that he dented the steering wheel and nearly took helmsman Jim Mattingly overboard with him. The RDF set vanished. Teddy Jr. sat on the windward side of the boat with his back to the rail and his feet wedged against the cabin top. Every now and again he would glance over his right shoulder and look up as far as he could crane his neck. All he could see was water. Having never encountered anything like it in his young life, he figured it was normal for this time and place. "Ignorance is bliss, I guess," he says. "I didn't have a parade of imaginary horrors yet. I thought this was cool."

When it got too rough to stay on deck, he went below. At about 8:00 a.m. Tuesday while breakfast was being served, *Tenacious* picked up the BBC Radio news. "That's when I knew how bad it was," Teddy says. "Everyone went quiet."

Nick DeGrazia says that the Ted Turner who was strutting around the docks in Plymouth was not the same man he came to know the following year. After the Fastnet, DeGrazia got to know Gary Jobson, one of Turner's watch captains, and over a drink in Plymouth, Jobson agreed to get him a place on *Tenacious* for the SORC races that winter. Finishing the Fastnet was as good a resume as it got. DeGrazia says Turner was a Jekyll and Hyde, hamming it up for the cameras and living up to his moniker as the Mouth from the South but becoming a totally different person once he left the dock.

"I liked him," DeGrazia says. "Ted was two different people. I found him a delight once he was on the boat and we were out to sea. He'd come down the dock and there was always media, cameras, and reporters, and he would show up with some devastatingly beautiful woman. You didn't feel he was part of the crew. But once he got on the boat, he was wonderful. He wanted to know all about you and how long you'd been racing and there were no egotistical remarks. He never talked about himself. It was about you and world events. I think he had an incredibly magic touch on the boat."

Turner's son Teddy adds, "My dad was a rock that night, and in those situations that's who you look to, to the leaders, either the natural ones, or the elected one. Dad always says what comes to his mind. But, hey, he's right, it is a rough ocean."


It was the Australians who, by virtue of a strong finish in the Fastnet, won the 1979 Admiral's Cup. Their captain, Syd Fischer, maintained in interviews that there was nothing unusual about the weather, saying that storms like that were encountered during the Sydney-Hobart race, the annual Boxing Day classic that runs 628 miles down the east coast of Australia from Sydney to Hobart, Tasmania. Almost twenty years later, during the 1998 running of that race, long after Fischer's comments were forgotten, they would become true. The sunny skies and moderate breezes for the first part of the race developed into gusts of eighty-five knots as a weather bomb lashed the fleet. Six people died, twenty-four boats were abandoned or sunk, and fifty-seven sailors were rescued.

Fischer said the worst of the storm had hit after he rounded Fastnet, where the wind was recorded at more than seventy knots. It was tough, with the visibility down to two hundred yards, but they did not stop racing.

Writing about the 1979 Fastnet Race nearly four years later, Jim Robson-Scott, a member of *Police Car's* crew, explained that Fischer's bravado stemmed from the Australians' greater experience with bad weather. Robson-Scott said Australians get equally bad storms in summer and winter. Since summer there lasts eight months, compared to half that in Western Europe, it stood to reason the Australians would experience more bad storms and learn how to sail in them. "It has been said that it's possible to do ten full seasons offshore in Britain without being exposed to a really bad blow," he said. "I wish that were true in Australia."

The rescue helicopters continued their search through Wednesday, but the sick bay at Culdrose was quiet. The airbase was inundated with calls from relatives anxious to hear news of the survivors, but the rescuers were having problems in locating the smaller craft because most of them did not have radio transmitters and were unable to report their position or condition.

The search was called off on Thursday, August 16, as Force 9 gales returned to the area. The tally by then was staggering: seventeen deaths, including two people from the trimaran *Bucks Fizz*, which had been following the race. The trimaran flipped at the height of the storm. Of the 303 yachts that started, 88 finished, less than 30 per cent. Some 24 boats were abandoned, although 19 of those were eventually recovered. Of 136 people rescued, all left the hospital. In Parliament, there was a call for a public inquiry. The Royal Ocean Racing Club started its own investigation.

The abandoned yachts were a windfall for Cornish fishermen, who temporarily abandoned their normal jobs to become salvors. Insurers would pay them one-third of the value of any yacht retrieved intact, a more lucrative catch than mackerel or skate.

The seven-man crew of the Falmouth Lifeboat returned to a hero's welcome after battling the gale for forty-four hours and saving nine lives. They were ordered to sea on Tuesday evening to search for survivors and did not return until lunchtime Thursday. During that time, their boat, the *Elizabeth Ann*, travelled 431 miles and used 1,000 gallons of fuel.

"It was hell, just hell out there," engineer Ron Twydle told the *Guardian*. "Those yachtsmen at the height of the storm could do nothing else but pray."

*Magistri* sailed into Plymouth mid-afternoon Wednesday after playing a cat-and-mouse game with Ted Heath's *Morning Cloud*. The weather had improved dramatically, and the last day was sailed with the spinnaker. It was as nice a day at sea as you could have: sunny, moderate winds, warm, everybody feeling good, clothes drying. As they came into Plymouth Sound, Chris Punter went below and came back on deck dressed in a tuxedo, clutching a bottle of Courvoisier, which he had tucked away and which had miraculously survived intact. He toasted the boat, the voyage, the adventure, his friends, and their survival.

Wearing his tuxedo, which somehow survived the Fastnet, Chris Punter regales Chuck Bentley with a poem at the dock in Plymouth.

(*Arch Alyea*)

*Magistri* drifted across the harbour on a dying breeze, beating the former British prime minister by thirteen minutes to claim twentieth place in the race. *Morning Cloud* came twenty-ninth on corrected time. Although *Morning Cloud* had rounded Fastnet four hours ahead of *Magistri*, she had lain ahull for several hours after her knockdown while *Magistri* kept sailing. That made all the difference.

There was an enormous sense of pride and personal achievement aboard the Canadian boat, the boat that nobody expected to win. *Magistri* had made it to England by the skin of her teeth and on a shoestring budget. "Nobody sailed with more heart than our group," Bentley says. "So to come out in the Fastnet and not only finish, but be the only Canadian finisher, we were pretty proud."

The crew was amazed by the mayhem in the basin, only later realizing that the excitement was for Heath, not them. Exhaustion and elation made their reunions with wives and girlfriends, some of the girlfriends acquaintances of just a few weeks, all a blur. A cork popped as they opened one of six bottles of champagne brought by John Bobyk, courtesy of Don Green. The rest of the *Evergreen* crew had scattered, and only Bobyk remained because he was still doing radio reports for CFRB Radio in Toronto. It was an emotionally charged party, the boats rafted out six and seven deep.

"I was very mellow, very satisfied, very proud," Nick DeGrazia says. "I felt very grateful, and I had a real sense of accomplishment. We had looked Mother Nature in the eye and survived. It was one of those events where you're pleased you had the experience, but you never want to do it again. It took me three days to get to London from Plymouth because we hit every pub along the way."

Bobyk was struck by how haunted the crew looked: red-rimmed, bloodshot eyes, cheeks scoured by wind and water, unshaven faces, and wild, tangled hair. They looked like ten miles of rough road. Bobyk knew how bad it had been when one of the crew, glass of champagne in hand, sat down and started to cry. "The emotions just poured out of him," Bobyk said.

The party eventually moved to the yacht club bar, where the *Evergreen* crew had been the night before. A reporter from the German news magazine *Der Stern* was looking for exclusive photos and had a suitcase full of money. Andre Calla sold a roll of unexposed film for almost $1,000 (U.S.) For a few hours, the elation endured, but one by one the crew drifted off. Chris Punter called home and spoke to his parents, who thought he was dead. The conversation took the edge off the celebration, as did a radio interview with a local Toronto station. Punter was tearful as the interviewer asked him the questions to which there was no answer. "When it hit, it was pretty profound," he says. "It gave me some perspective on how quick and fleeting life can be, how we don't have control over things."

In the early hours of Wednesday, Peter Whipp was wandering naked in his sleep down the cobbled streets of Plymouth Hoe, chased by the warden of the seaman's mission and by Tim Allison. All of Plymouth's hotels had been booked for the expected arrival of the Fastnet fleet, and the *Magic* crew had spent only the first night in a hotel. The second night, they moved to the mission. Whipp had had horrible nightmares the previous night and now they had returned. Allison awoke to hear him shouting and then saw his friend amble out the front door and down the street. The warden ran after him, shouting as well. Allison followed and together they retrieved Whipp and put him back to bed. Next morning, he had only a vague memory of what happened.

For the next four or five months, Whipp had nightmares involving drowning at sea. *Magic* was sinking or he was watching her float away and was unable to swim the gap. More than once, his frightened wife, then pregnant with twins, had to shake him awake as he tried to push the bed out the door because "the anchor was dragging."

Whipp was clearly suffering from post-traumatic stress disorder and he was not the only one. During interviews for this book, several other survivors of the race were close to tears while describing the events more than a quarter-century ago. The memories brought back the dread and terror they experienced all those years ago.

For months afterwards, Peter Milligan dreamed about the race. In the dreams, the boat was sunk, he and his friends were drowning, and he was utterly helpless. The dreams woke him up in the middle of the night and left him sweating and gasping for breath. A few months after the end of the race, Jim Talmage was walking across the campus of McMaster University in Hamilton on a cold and blustery night. "All of a sudden I was back in that race," he says. "I got home and the phone rang and it was Dennis Aggus. He said, 'Do you know how windy it is out there tonight?' I said, 'Yes' and then he said, 'What are you thinking about?' I said, 'Probably the same things you are.'"

Aggus had been putting his garbage out on the curb when the wind blew up his shirt, triggering the memory of lying on his stomach operating the engine controls during the attempt to rescue *Magic*. "That cold icy finger of doom was on my back, and I remember thinking, Boy, we were lucky," he says. "We *were* lucky."

A week after the race, Stewart Jones broke out in unexplained boils on his back and chest. "Big, huge, ugly-looking things the size of a loonie," he says. "I'm sure it was stress. It was like toxin coming out." Just as mysteriously as they erupted, they went away.

On the morning after his radio interview, Chris Punter attended a memorial service for the sailors who had perished and felt an emotional catharsis. The service at St. Andrew's Anglican Church, the large downtown cathedral in Plymouth, wove together all the emotions of the race: fear for his life, sorrow for the dead, humility before the power of the sea, and the feeling that his survival was sheer luck. The service was packed; all the pews were filled. The Bishop of Plymouth read Psalm 107, often called the Sailor's Psalm:

*Those who go down to the sea in ships,*
*Who do business on great waters,*
*They see the works of the Lord,*
*And His wonders in the deep . . .*

*Then they cry out to the Lord in their trouble,*
*And He brings them out of their distresses.*
*He calms the storm,*
*So that its waves are still.*
*Then they are glad because they are quiet;*
*So He guides them to their desired haven.*

"I bawled my eyes out, and I think that was my saving grace," Punter said. "I deal with a lot of traumatic stress in my work: homicides and what police officers go through. It was an absolute catharsis. I didn't have any sleeping problems."

Among those who claimed to suffer no aftereffects, a few things suggested otherwise. Glenn Shugg had an unopened copy of John Rousmaniere's *Fastnet, Force 10* on his bookshelf for ten years. "I couldn't read it, I didn't want to go there," he says. Peter Whipp has never read any account of the race.

It took Don Green a few days to unwind. In the first twenty-four hours, he did several interviews with Canadian newspapers, TV, and radio, all the time feeling alone and a long way from home, isolated, frustrated, and helpless. Today, when he thinks back to the race, he seems to judge himself harshly, although he does not articulate what exactly he feels he failed to do. Sometimes when he's outside in high winds, Green's mind replays the many variables and he feels lucky. "You appreciate the sun coming up in the morning and going down at night and the beautiful things around you. We were so very fortunate."

Al Megarry says the race was a life-changing event, but it didn't put him off sailing, as he has since gone on to spend every spare moment ocean racing. He's competed in six Canada's Cups – and won four – an America's Cup, and most of the big offshore races along the Eastern Seaboard. Megarry suffered no ill aftereffects, though he is convinced that in that one race, he used up three of his nine lives. He felt good about the way he handled himself. "I stepped it up a notch. Not many Canadians have done that race, and I'm proud that I was one of those guys. I didn't finish, but I was there."

Peter Cowern already thought of himself as a pretty hardy fellow and came away with a new understanding of how deep his reserves were. "When you go through tough experiences, you dig deep to keep going," he says. "You realize that if you put your mind to it, you can do anything you want."

No one seems to have been put off ocean racing. Many aboard *Magistri* competed in the 1983 race with Peter Farlinger, including Andre Calla, Fred Goode, Peter Cowern, and Peter Milligan. That year the Canadians came fifth in the Admiral's Cup, with *Magistri* leading the team and winning the cross-Channel race. It was a light-air series, her kind of wind. Many of *Pachena*'s crew entered the race twice more with skipper John Newton, in 1981 when the Canadians came sixth and again in 1985 when they were thirteenth.

After what they suffered in 1979, why would they want to do it again?

Fred Goode tries to explain the enduring attraction of the race: "At Cowes, there's a thousand boats coming down the Solent with chutes up. It's mind-boggling."

# *16*

# *Lessons*

**"It is not the critic who counts, not the man who points out how the strong man stumbles. . . . The credit belongs to the man who . . . strives valiantly . . . and who if he fails at least fails while daring greatly."**

– THEODORE ROOSEVELT

*A* FEW DAYS after the end of the race, the Canadian crews drifted off in pairs or alone to explore parts of England and put some distance between themselves and the race. The Greens and Fitzpatricks toured the southwest of England. Alan Jeyes, Jim Talmage, and Al Megarry rented a car and went to visit Jeyes's brother-in-law, a submarine commander. The Killings ended up at a bed and breakfast on Dartmoor, where long hikes restored Steve's emotional equilibrium. Dave Downey dismantled *Evergreen*. She was put on a container and shipped back to Canada as deck cargo. Don Green never set foot on her again.

Arch Alyea went to Land's End at the southwestern tip of Cornwall to see for himself the condition of the boats that had been towed in and salvaged. He took pictures to show everyone back home, just in case they didn't believe him. Nick DeGrazia wobbled up to London one pub at a time, and so what was normally a three-hour train ride took three days. Chris Punter visited family. Fred Goode and his wife flew to Portugal for a holiday. As luck would have it, Goode ended up with a severe case of food poisoning and flew back to London, where he spent a week in bed. Between that and the race, he lost ten pounds. Dennis Hogarth sailed *Magistri* back across the Atlantic to Antigua, where she was overhauled and readied for a winter of racing, including Antigua Race Week and the 1980 Miami-Nassau SORC race.

John Newton left *Pachena* in Crosshaven and flew to London, where his wife was waiting. Some of *Pachena's* crew left as quickly as they could get flights, but Steve Tupper, Doug Race, and Stewart Jones stayed on for a few days as guests of Ron Holland. Finally, only Jones was left to put together a crew to get *Pachena* back to Plymouth. From there, he sailed down the Channel, up the east coast of Britain, across the North Sea to the Oslo Fjord, and then along the coast to Porsgrund, Norway. The voyage only brought more storms. During the trip from Cork to Plymouth, he ran into gale-force winds, and breaking waves filled the cockpit at least three times, and for two days in the North Sea *Pachena* beat into fifty-knot winds with three reefs in her main and a tiny jib. "It was unbelievable," Jones says. "It never ended that summer."

In Norway, *Pachena* was put in a container, loaded on to a freighter, and shipped back to Vancouver.


A few days after the race, at a press conference in Plymouth, the race organizers defended their decision to start the race despite the iffy long-range forecast, claiming that the disaster was the result of conditions that they could not have predicted. Alan Green, secretary of the Royal Ocean Racing Club, was unequivocal in absolving the RORC from all blame.

"Once the race has started – unless there are exceptional circumstances – there is no means of communication with the boats," he said. "This is well known in the sport. The boats are entirely self-sufficient and the owners completely understand that this is the case.

"They have prepared their boats in the best possible way and it is their responsibility to judge the weather and to take such action as it occurs to them is right. There is no way the race committee can say, 'Stop, go home.' It cannot be done."

Green said that the race's record since 1925 spoke for itself and called what had happened this year "a freak." When asked about the future of the sport, he said, "I do not believe that when accidents happen a sport is going to stop." He also said that the club had already started an investigation, jointly with the national sailing body, the Royal Yachting Association.

Five months later, in January 1980, the results of their investigation were made public. The inquiry's report was based on a questionnaire sent to all competitors, with about 80 per cent of the yachts responding. It looked at the weather, examined the ability of the boats and their equipment to withstand the storm, considered whether crew experience was a factor, and evaluated the search-and-rescue operation.

The report unequivocally deflated the notion that the storm had been worst over the Labadie Bank, an area where many of the rescues had taken place. Because the water was somewhat shallower over the bank, many sailors believed it created a shoreline effect that aggravated the effects of the storm. There was no proof of this, the report said.

The race was compared to 1957, the other bad storm year. Statistically, they were similar in some ways. In 1957, twelve of forty-one boats finished, just 29 per cent of the fleet. In 1979, there were eight times as many boats, but the same percentage of finishers.

Not surprisingly, the report exonerated the race committee for starting the race and for not calling it off when the storm hit, echoing what Alan Green had said five months earlier. It said that since forecasts are issued only for the next twenty-four hours, organizers could not have known with any certainty what lay ahead. When the committee did know, it was too late. Even so, the decision to set sail or abandon a race lay with the skippers.

"The arrival of Force 8 gales with little warning is a feature of our weather which all who sail must expect to encounter from time to time," the report continued. "No ocean racing skipper would regard such a wind as involving conditions which would ordinarily dictate the abandonment of the race."

While the inquiry concluded that the light weight of some yachts may have caused them to broach sooner, or more often, it did not make any recommendation about the design of yachts. Ultimately, the report implied, the boats had stood up well, even those that had been abandoned; it was the people who buckled.

George Cuthbertson, president of C&C Yachts, told the *Toronto Star* there was no logic in blaming the disaster on lighter boats. Yachts built to Admiral's Cup standards and operated by efficient crews should be capable of withstanding stormy seas, he said. "Some people talk about fragile, delicate racing boats. They imply that cruise boats are sound, husky, sturdier vessels, which take more punishment. The reverse is actually true. The racing boat is sailed far harder and pushed far beyond what a cruising boat is called on to do. Because a boat is lighter doesn't mean it's weaker. Aircraft designers for years have striven for lightness. New space-age materials make this possible without sacrificing strength."

The report found two areas where safety could be improved. They recommended that subsequent fleets have larger diameter cockpit drains, so breaking seas could drain faster. They also recommended the addition of watertight compartments, so that should the boats be overwhelmed they would not sink. These two recommendations were later adopted by the ocean-racing fraternity. In solo around-the-world races such as the Vendée Globe, boats must have three watertight compartments and be able to float with two of them damaged.

There was a recommendation that boats carry hacksaws or another means of cutting away rigging in an emergency to stop it from becoming a hazard. This has also been universally adopted. The report also suggested that harness webbing be of a minimum strength and that attachment points be firm. These points, too, are now standard requirements for ocean races.

The report talked about shortcomings in the design and strength of the life rafts and the weather protection they afforded. The rafts were not, as many believed, safer than the yachts. "That was one of the great lessons," Nick DeGrazia says. "You're safer in a watertight container with no mast. Nail the hatches shut or screw them shut if you have to, but never step down into a life raft."

The report found no conclusive evidence that the level of experience of the skippers had a bearing on the number of knockdowns, abandonments, or on the loss of life. Nevertheless, it recommended that the RORC consider whether qualifications should be required for long ocean races. The club adopted this, and for the next race, crews had to have accomplished a minimum number of ocean races to be eligible. Another recommendation it adopted was the requirement that all boats have radios that could send and receive.

Ron Barr says that had these rules been applied in 1979, *Evergreen* would not have been eligible because the crew had too little experience of ocean racing. But, he asks, who *was* trained for those conditions, as the only way to get heavy-weather sailing experience is to sail in heavy weather. That is why the Australians won. They have experience sailing in heavy weather. *Evergreen's* designer, Rob Ball, says, "We were hoping for a light air series because we were all light air sailors. If you put us over there with heavy air sailors, in light air we'd kill 'em, even if we were racing in a bathtub. But on a heavy air day we were just trying to hang on and stay upright, and those guys were picking their wind shift."

During the storm, some boats lay ahull, with no sail up, others hove to with a small sail counterbalancing the rudder, and a third group ran off before the storm with or without sail. The investigators examined these tactics to see if any one tactic was better than the other. When Adlard Coles tackled this question in *Heavy Weather Sailing*, his conclusion was that the key to avoiding a knockdown or worse is to have enough control to manoeuvre. He defined "control" as sufficient speed for the helmsman to bear off, come up, or scoot around the worst of waves.

This control might be under bare poles or with a storm jib or any combination of sail that the crew deemed appropriate. Coles noted that a majority of small-boat sailors treated the conditions as a survival storm – not surprisingly – and adopted normal gale tactics of heaving to and lying ahull. A survey of the fleet after the race showed that the largest proportion lay ahull.

There are many methods of heaving to, but all involve pointing the bow into the weather and balancing the force of the sails against the rudder so that the boat remains stationary. Author Derek Lundy has described it as one of the elegant rituals that sailors have used for centuries to sit tight while they wait out bad weather, sleep, navigate, or make repairs. The change in motion is enormously calming. The banging and bouncing subsides and so does the noise, which is perhaps the most unnerving element of a storm. A boat can stay this way indefinitely if it has enough sea room, for it will gradually drift to leeward. The problem arises when the wind gets too strong and the waves too high and the boat can no longer balance the forces. The boat may surge forward, and if waves are sweeping the deck, the motion can become dangerous, particularly if the waves are close to together, as they were in the Irish Sea.

Lying ahull is a variation of heaving to. Again, the bow is pointed into the wind, but the sail is not balanced against the rudder. You lock yourself up, go below and pray. About 30 per cent of the fleet did that, reporting that while there was plenty of noise and even a few broaches, it was effective. One skipper who lay ahull for fifteen hours dryly noted that it was safe and stable. "The greatest hazard [is] a rollover, which is acceptable under the circumstances."

About 36 per cent of yachts reported running off before the storm and half of those used warps to slow their boat down. These days, the idea that a fast-moving boat is safer in heavy weather is widely accepted, especially when satellite weather forecasts and the age of wireless Internet can provide accurate pictures of developing systems. The faster the boat, the better the chance of getting out of harm's way. You have control, an ability to manoeuvre, the rudder is more responsive, and the split-second decisions can be made with more certainty of success. That's the theory, anyway.

The notion that one could safely run off before a survival storm was tested by single-hander Bernard Moitessier in 1965 during one of his circumnavigations. He ran before one particular monster in the Southern Ocean and threw some ropes out behind the boat, hoping their drag would slow him down and keep the stern square to the rollers. He reasoned that if he could maintain a steady speed, he could steer clear of the worst of it. It seemed to work. Later in the voyage, he encountered an even bigger storm and adopted the same tactics. He almost pitch-poled because he was moving too fast. By chance, he took a wave a little off the stern, on the quarter, and noticed an immediate improvement. Recalling that the Argentine single-hander Vito Dumas had done something similar, Moitessier cut his ropes free and ran before the storm, which raged for six full days.

The report said there was no consensus about which storm tactics worked best – running, heaving to, or laying ahull – but it did observe that there was "a general inference that active rather than passive tactics were successful." For most of the fleet, the conditions were outside the realm of previous experience, so mistakes were inevitable. Even so, the report noted, "the general standards of seamanship, navigation and certainly courage, were commendably high."

The Canadian boats represented radically different designs. *Magistri*, the oldest and heaviest, finished, mainly because by going west early Monday it ended up at a good angle to round Fastnet. *Pachena* was also a heavy, well-built boat, and could have finished had she not been off course. *Evergreen* made the wise decision to abandon the race, yet Steve Killing maintains that the boat's light weight worked in her favour, as she slid sideways when slammed by waves rather than resisting their full force.

"A lot was written afterwards about whether design was moving in the wrong direction," he says. "Being beamy and light means you get blown around a lot, but you also skid a lot. Skidding is better than tipping." The design of the open transom also helped, as it allowed water to flow out of the boat quickly, permitting *Evergreen* to rise and stagger on before a second blow could knock her out.

For designer Rob Ball, this was a vindication. Before the race, he says, "There was a lot of criticism that the open transom was unsafe. But it turned out that, in those conditions, it was a lot safer than a closed one."

The report concluded that "the sea showed it can be a deadly enemy and that those who go to sea for pleasure must do so in the full knowledge that they may encounter dangers of the highest order. However, provided the lessons so harshly taught in this race are well learned, we feel the yachts should continue to race over the Fastnet course again."

The report's findings offered the sailing press plenty of opportunity for analysis and interpretation, but the popular press had long since moved on. There was revolution in Iran, the Soviets had invaded Afghanistan, and the West planned to boycott the 1980 Moscow Games. The new man in the White House was Hollywood actor Ronald Reagan.

Undeterred, or perhaps encouraged by the report, a record six boats posted $14,000 performance bonds with the Canadian Yachting Association in November 1980. They were vying for the three spots on the 1981 Admiral's Cup team. The Fastnet that year attracted 250 boats, 200 of them crewed by eager amateurs. This was fifty fewer than 1979, but still an impressive turnout. New rules meant the skippers and at least half the crew had to have sailed in two offshore races in the previous twelve months. All boats were required to have two-way radios. A pre-race safety inspection was mandatory.

In light winds, *Kialoa* avenged her 1979 second-place finish by crossing the line first in Plymouth in 1980. Britain restored her honour by winning the Admiral's Cup. The weekend sailors got the challenging and exciting ride they hoped for with none of the danger. All was well.

Perhaps that is the lesson. The sea is never the same, not from one day to the next, let alone one year to another. By turns beautiful and terrifying, unpredictable and dangerous, it has always attracted the adventurers willing to take up its challenge. And while they expect the best, they should prepare for the worst, because ability and experience can be swept aside if you are unlucky enough to be in the wrong place at the wrong time. It is something the 303 crews in the 1979 Fastnet learned the hard way, and something wise sailors bear in mind when they leave a safe harbour in a small boat to do battle with the sea.

# *Afterword*

**"Experience: that most brutal of teachers. But you learn,
my God do you learn."**

– C.S. LEWIS

*D*ON GREEN'S HOME is on North Shore Boulevard in Burlington,
Ontario, a winding road where tall hedges hide sculpted gardens
and the wrought-iron gates have electronic buzzers and locks.
Green's estate is nestled beside one of the greens of the Burlington
Golf and Country Club, and his patio looks onto Hamilton Harbour,
where on a breezy early September day boats flit back and forth in
a slight chop on the bay.

Green is dressed casually in blue slacks and a short-sleeved shirt,
the handshake firm and friendly. He guides a visitor to his study, a
place which in many ways is a shrine to the eighteen months when
*Evergreen* was the woman in his life.

Leather wingback chairs flank either side of the fireplace, and
above it, *Evergreen* is sailing downwind in an oil painting, with spinnaker and blooper flying. Behind his desk is a photo of *Evergreen* in

the Solent, a young Al Megarry, his hair flying, resplendent in his white foul-weather gear with a choirboy's angelic grin. Beside that is a photo of *Evergreen* on Lake Ontario. There is a model of her hull on the wall.

He looks intently at the photos for a moment, then turns and says, "It was a terrible boat to sail. Terrible. It was out of control most of the time."

Exactly a week to the day after the Fastnet race started, most of the *Evergreen* crew flew home together from London. Green put the boat up for sale with the condition that the new owner change the name and the boat could not be raced on the Great Lakes. He wanted nothing more to do with her.

A doctor in Long Island bought her, but when he unwrapped the mast and had a closer look, he asked for an adjustment on the sale price. The mast had a lot of wrinkles in it, "all kinds of twists and turns," Green says. He does not know who bought the boat, only that the new owner was never happy with it.

"I suppose it's lying in some yard now."

Green was glad to see the boat go and figures the mast was not far from a stress fracture, one big gust away from a dismasting. But he also loves the boat because it brought him glory and allowed him to participate in a once-in-a-lifetime experience. He regrets now not knowing what happened to her, because ultimately, for all her weaknesses, *Evergreen* was strong and safe and cared for her crew.

Green was named to the Order of Canada in 1980. He built another *Evergreen*, a forty-five-footer designed by German Frers in California. He kept it in Ft. Lauderdale, where for the next few years he raced in the Florida winter circuit, side by side with Ted Turner. He continued to nurture the dream that Canada could become a player at the highest levels of ocean racing, seeing such an endeavour as a force for national unity.

In 1984, he announced his plans for the *True North* syndicate, aiming for a Canadian challenge for the 1985 America's Cup to be held in Australia. His old foe from the 1978 Canada's Cup, Paul Phelan, was among the first to come on board. Peter Farlinger signed on as director of operations. Al Megarry was part of the crew. Steve Killing was the designer. A second syndicate based in Calgary and headed by lawyer Marvin McDill launched its own challenge, called *Canada II*, and with both syndicates bleeding, they merged. Only one boat could go to the Cup and after trials it was *Canada II* that went, not *True North*. *Canada II* disappointed and finished ninth of thirteen teams.

For Green, that was it. His business needed his full-time help as the global auto industry was rapidly changing. He eventually sold the company and, today at age seventy-one, remains active on the boards of several start-up companies and was recently chairman of McMaster University in Hamilton, Ontario.

In December 1980, Kodak Canada transferred Dennis Aggus to British Columbia and he gave up sailing. The Fastnet, he says, "was something to endure. You met the worst the sea can throw at you and you managed to survive." The highlight of his racing career remains the 1978 Canada's Cup campaign.

When Ron Barr's plane touched down in Toronto, friends picked him up, threw his bags in the back, and instead of heading home they drove to the Burlington Sailing and Boating Club. It was race night. He doesn't remember how he placed. It didn't matter.

Barr was recently commodore of the Burlington Sailing and Boating Club. He believes he is alive today because on *Evergreen* they did the right things at the right time. "We hadn't been through anything like that, but we knew how to meet a challenge and endure," he says.

Steve Killing has become one of Canada's premier yacht designers. He designed the *Express 30* and then the *Express 20* and *35*. In 1983, he co-designed Canada's first entry in the America's Cup, *Canada I*, along with Bruce Kirkby. Two years later, he designed *True North* for Don Green. Killing continued his big boat designs, working on the 1988 New Zealand America's Cup challenge that lost to Dennis Conner's *Stars & Stripes*. Killing lives in Midland, Ontario, on Georgian Bay and enjoys dinghy racing, in a Fusion 15, a boat that he designed. Like *Evergreen*, the Fusion 15 has an open transom at the stern.

Al Megarry was a member of Canada's America's Cup challenge in 1983 and again in 1985. Megarry is valued on the race circuit, and he has invitations to go just about everywhere a rich man needs an A-list sailor. He has no intention of buying a boat. "Why, when I am fortunate to be invited onto the best boats all over the world?"

Megarry maintains that a lot of boats got into trouble in 1979 because they took sails down and sat it out. *Evergreen* was always moving reasonably quickly so had some steerage and control.

Jim Talmage did the 1981 Canada's Cup aboard *Coug*. Two years later, he did the winter Onion Patch races in Bermuda. And then there were no challenges left for him. "I'd been part of the best racing programs ever put together. What was I going to do? Wednesday-night club races?"

Everyone lost touch with Alan Jeyes, the navigator. After a battle with Alzheimer's, John Fitzpatrick died in December 2005, at the age of seventy-one. Many of the *Evergreen* crew reunited at his memorial service, the first time they had all been together since August 1979.

Peter Whipp, Peter Hoosen-Owen, and Tim Allison remain friends, live in the Isle of Man, and still sail. Whipp built two more racing forty-footers, both called *Panda*. He raced in the 1985 Fastnet as part of the British Admiral's Cup team and won on corrected time. The weather had in many ways been a reminder of 1979. That Christmas, he took *Panda* to Australia for his second Sydney-Hobart. After a day at sea, it looked as if he had a chance to win there too.

Mid-afternoon on that second day, as *Panda* was beating into twenty-five knots of southerly wind, she came off the top of an irregular wave. In the 1979 Fastnet, boats were being tossed around like this every few minutes for hours on end in conditions that were far worse. *Panda* landed with a thud and the inner laminates of the hull, where they were attached to the keel, peeled part. Whipp believes that had the thin outer skin gone as well, the yacht would have instantly sunk. He abandoned the race and nursed the boat to shore.

He gave up offshore racing in 1986, when, like John Newton, he felt the day of the amateur was over. "The thing was turning professional and there was a lot of cheating going on," Whipp says. "I race Lasers now, believe it or not."

And races them quite well. In the fall of 2005, Whipp was in Brazil at the Laser World Championships. He came fifth in the Masters class – for those fifty-five and over. He was disappointed. He had come third the year earlier in Turkey.

Allison laments that his last decent sail was in 1996, but says it's hard to take the time off from his 300-acre beef farm. Peter Hoosen-Owen taught for many years and then moved into administration, eventually becoming the principal of a grammar school in Ramsay. He gave up ocean racing after the Fastnet, but continued to do coastal sailing. He was recently principal of the Royal Yachting Association training establishment on Man, which teaches children to sail. He feels a tight bond of comradeship with his two friends, "an invisible thing."

Since 1979, Chuck Bentley has led a vagabond's life as a professional skipper. He was aboard *Coug* with Al Megarry for the 1980 Canada's Cup, worked at a sail loft briefly, and returned to the Admiral's Cup in 1981 and 1985. For five years, he was the skipper of a seventy-foot ketch, running the boat for a wealthy American family. After his benefactor died, the boat was sold and Bentley landed a new job as skipper of a 123-foot ketch owned by a California oil man. These days he lives in St. Petersburg, Florida.

Bentley bought a Santana 525 in California, a daysailer that he painted in the same colours and with the same graphics as *Magistri*. At the time of writing, it hadn't been in the water for about six years and the bottom needed a new coat of epoxy. But with time on his hands, Bentley plans to do the work.

Some years after the Fastnet, Bentley sailed though a hurricane while crossing the Atlantic. The wind might have been as strong, but the waves didn't have time to build. "In my sailing, never did I encounter the same seas again," he says.

For Arch Alyea, the Fastnet was the last of big stuff for him and remains a cherished moment. "I felt a tremendous sense of pride, having been there, done that, and survived," he says. "It is one of the memorable events of my life."

He lives in Cambridge, Ontario, and owns a Mega 30, an early C&C design that he keeps on Lake Erie at the Port Dover Yacht Club.

Andre Calla went back for the 1983 Admiral's Cup with Peter Farlinger. In 1985, he acted as manager for the Canadian team.

He lives in Toronto, has continued to sail when he can, and is a member of the Royal Ocean Racing Club and the Royal Canadian Yacht Club. The 1979 Fastnet holds a special place for him, as do the people he sailed with. "I learned a lot about the importance of friends," he says. "We were all in it together and we all looked after one another and that's all that matters."

Peter Cowern was part of Peter Farlinger's 1983 Admiral's Cup team. In the intervening years, Cowern has tried parachuting and enjoys scuba diving. He sailed in one Newport-to-Bermuda race and has cruised in the Caribbean. "I came out of it thinking I was a tougher person than when I started," he says of the Fastnet.

In the winter of 1980, Nicholas DeGrazia did the Florida series on *Tenacious* with Ted Turner. He left teaching for administration, and in 1990, he became president of the toy company Lionel Trains. These days you can find him about twelve miles north of Point Huron, Michigan, where he has opened a bed and breakfast with his wife. He has a fifteen-foot Point Jude sailboat, a green-hulled little thing with red sails and teak trim. He's thinking of buying a forty-foot catamaran and living on it. He never sailed with the *Magistri* crew again.

Fred Goode lives in Margaret's Bay, Nova Scotia, outside of Halifax, not far from Peggy's Cove. The house has the ocean on three sides, and he bought it when he retired from the RCMP in 1989. Just forty-five, he started an office stationery company and retired for a second time in 2004, just shy of his sixtieth birthday.

Goode was part of Peter Farlinger's 1983 team and did four SORC winter series, but he never really liked ocean racing. In the winter of 2005, he went heli-skiing in B.C., taking a helicopter ride up twelve thousand feet and spending a day getting to the bottom. He was petrified and compares the experience to the 1979 Fastnet.

A year after the Fastnet, Peter Farlinger bought the old *Magistri* from her five other owners and traded it in at C&C Yachts against a new C&C 39 *Magistri*, which was put in the water in early 1982. (C&C sold the 1979 Admiral's Cup *Magistri* to a member of Toronto's National Yacht Club. For some years, her new owner did very well in regattas along the lake.)

Farlinger returned to England for the Admiral's Cup in 1983. He says the prime motivation for returning was because the team wanted to prove that with a fast boat they were contenders. This time, the conditions were perfect – a light air series in which *Magistri* won the cross-Channel race, the only time a Canadian boat has come first in any Admiral's Cup event.

The conditions were so gentle the crew was hard-pressed to keep the boat moving as it rounded Fastnet Rock. It was the same place on the chart, but it was an entirely different experience. The rounding was in bright sunshine on a lovely warm day, with the boat ghosting along with everyone working hard to keep the spinnaker full. "It was surreal," Farlinger says.

The series was a lot of fun but didn't stack up to 1979. But then again, what could? "The race in 1979 was an experience of a lifetime," Farlinger says.

*Magistri* did so well it caught the eye of the well-heeled racing set. Two members of Sweden's most famous family of industrialists and diplomats, the Wallenbergs, purchased it. Farlinger undertook to help them deliver the boat to Stockholm.

Farlinger sailed competitively for a few more years and managed the America's Cup challenge for Don Green. After that, he gave it up. These days, Farlinger lives in Owen Sound, Ontario.

Farlinger often returns to a moment in the race, at about 4:00 a.m. on Tuesday, August 14, when *Magistri* was trying to round Fastnet and the lives of her crew were very much in doubt. Their fate hinged on the strength of some metal part that might or might not fail, or a line that was about to snap, or an error in his judgment as he steered through the storm. Any one of those events and a dozen others could have led to their death.

"Yet, it was an extraordinarily beautiful place to be," he says. "My biggest fear is a belief that I will never see anything as beautiful as that again."

John Hollidge became disenchanted with ocean racing – too many electronic aids meant the art of navigation was being lost – and he gave it up in 1984. Hollidge's career has thrived and 2006 found him living in Rome, where he was the British naval and air attaché in Italy and defence adviser to Malta.

Peter Milligan is a Toronto property taxation and assessment lawyer. He no longer sails but is the part owner of a forty-two-foot powerboat that he keeps at the Royal Canadian Yacht Club.

"There are times when all the preparation in the world won't help you," he says about the Fastnet. "I didn't think I was lucky, I just think it wasn't my time."

Chris Punter made his career as a criminal prosecutor in Toronto. These days, he owns four dinghies, which are raced with great enthusiasm by his four children. Punter reflects as often as not on the sense of comradeship he feels for the crew of the 1979 *Magistri*.

"I've sailed with a lot of people, and there's not many I'd choose to go back and sail with. I'd like to think these guys felt the same way. There was a trust and a bond. It was a unique time in our lives, unique and remarkable."

In 1981, John Newton's *Pachena* did well and the Canadians looked good, but in the 1985 Fastnet with the same boat, they were hopelessly outclassed. Newton was not accustomed to losing and decided enough was enough.

To perk himself up, he splurged on a fifty-four-footer, "absolutely gorgeous with all the bell's and whistles." He sailed that *Pachena* up and down the Pacific Northwest for ten years. That has since been traded in for a seventy-six-foot powerboat. He keeps *Princess Pachena* at the Royal Vancouver Yacht Club's Coal Harbour basin.

"We want to do Alaska, it's the last frontier," he says. In the spring of 2006, Newton was dissatisfied with her original length and added two more, bringing her to seventy-eight feet.

Stewart Jones went back to England with John Newton for the Fastnet in 1981, but the event didn't have the same electricity for him. For the past seventeen years, he has owned a mast and rigging shop in North Vancouver. In 2005, he was commodore of the West Vancouver Yacht Club and that year bought his first boat, a C&C 38. He plans to cruise in Howe Sound and among the many islands dotting the B.C. coast.

Don Martin, like Steve Killing, is the rare Canadian to make a living designing boats. Martin lives in Vancouver, and his best-selling design is the Martin 242, a smaller racer-cruiser that has a class association and is popular in British Columbia, California, and Japan. Some three hundred have been produced.

The Martin 16, a boat for disabled sailors, was in the running for the Beijing Paralympics, but lost in the end to an Australian design. Martin coached the Canadian paralympic team in 2002 and 2006.

He says he went to the 1979 Fastnet because it offered a sense of adventure. Despite the wretched night at sea, he also enjoyed himself in a perverse way. "I learned the value of determination and that you can do more than you think you can. That's a huge lesson."



Doug Race went back in 1981, with designer Bruce Kirkby on *Runaway*. Race has continued to sail and reckons he has done thirty-five Swiftsures. For many years, he raced a C&C 33 in Squamish, B.C., where he has a law firm. He has done several ocean crossings and has experienced plenty of bad weather, but Race says nothing holds a candle to the 1979 Fastnet. "I'd seen big waves, but never that much wind. It taught me that even though we had a life raft, never leave the boat unless the water is up around your nose."



Mike Schnetzler went back with John Newton in 1985, but didn't enjoy the race. The boat was old, the weather was similar to, though not as bad as in, 1979, and *Pachena* did just as badly. "I'd had enough at that point," Schnetzler said.

Schnetzler says the 1979 race, while challenging and frustrating, did not leave him in fear for his life. "In those situations, you do what you have to do," he says. "You look after yourself and the people around you and get on with it."

Glenn Shugg has never owned a sailboat but is a member at the Royal Vancouver Yacht Club and is heavily involved in its junior sailing program. Like Schnetzler, Shugg did not feel in ultimate peril during the 1979 Fastnet. "Was I scared? Yeah. You should be in those conditions."

John Simonett was part of the 1981 *Pachena* team, but that was it. "I have realized for quite some time I wouldn't have wanted to miss it. It was a great experience, not fun at the time, frightening, but not paralyzing. I wouldn't have missed it for the world."

Steve Tupper joined the Canadian Yachting Association in the fall of 1979 and was named coach of Canada's Olympic sailing team for the 1980 Games to be held in Moscow. Then Canada boycotted the Games. He was brought aboard Canada's first America's Cup program as a coach and later he joined BC Sailing, the provincial sport authority, as executive director.

John Newton sold *Pachena* to a sailor in the Vancouver area. She was sold again, and Stewart Jones saw her not long ago tied up at a dock in Seattle with the same temporary mast he had helped rig more than a quarter-century ago. Like his memories, the mast remains a vivid reminder of great events long ago.

# Acknowledgements

This book could not have been possible without the gracious cooperation of the people I interviewed at great length. Many of them were sailors during the 1979 Fastnet experience and all were involved in the event. They shared the intimate details of those intense, dramatic few days in the Irish Sea almost thirty years ago, and for many of them, reliving the race was not easy. All were generous with their time and patient with the many questions their stories elicited, and I thank them all.

I especially want to express my thanks and appreciation to Don Green, who gave me the names and current phone numbers of his crew. Thanks, too, to Andre Calla, for his exuberance was inspiring and his introductions opened many doors. Arch Alyea graciously made his photos available for the book, as did Andre, Stewart, and Boudina Jones; John Simonett, Sharon Green, and Steve Killing. Stewart's hospitality during a West Coast visit included a memorable slide show of race photos shown against the backdrop of the incomparably beautiful West Vancouver Yacht Club. Stewart and Andre kindly loaned me original newspaper and magazine articles about the race, as did Ann Bobyk, whose voluminous, orderly collection would make any archivist proud.

My wife, Leigh, was again my sounding board. Bill Comeau and David Cyr read the manuscript and their comments improved it immeasurably. All writers need a good editor. Mine was Dinah Forbes.

# Appendix 1

## 1979 Fastnet Race Results*

| POSITION | YACHT | COUNTRY |
|---|---|---|
| 1 | *Tenacious* | U.S.A. |
| 2 | *Eclipse* | Britain |
| 3 | *Jubilee VI* | France |
| 4 | *Revolootion* | France |
| 5 | *Impetuous* | Australia |
| 6 | *Police Car* | Australia |
| 7 | *Imp* | U.S.A. |
| 8 | *Condor of Bermuda* | Britain |
| 9 | *Kialoa* | U.S.A. |
| 10 | *Schollevoer* | Holland |

* Corrected time. Actual time adjusted for a handicap based on boat length.

# Appendix 2

## Canada's 1979 Admiral's Cup Performance

| RACE | *Evergreen* | *Magistri* | *Pachena* |
| --- | --- | --- | --- |
| *1<sup>st</sup> Inshore* | | | |
| Date: Wed., Aug. 1 | 37$^{th}$ | 41$^{st}$ | 48$^{th}$ |
| Distance: 30 miles | | | |
| Winds: W 8–25 knots | | | |
| | | | |
| *2<sup>nd</sup> Inshore* | | | |
| Date: Thurs., Aug. 2 | 46$^{th}$ | 52$^{nd}$ | 47$^{th}$ |
| Distance: 29 miles | | | |
| Winds: SW 13–30 knots | | | |
| | | | |
| *Channel Race[1]* | | | |
| Date: Fri., Aug. 3 | 34$^{th}$ | 36$^{th}$ | 24$^{th}$ |
| Distance: 217 miles | | | |
| Winds: W-SW 25 knots, then NW 15 knots | | | |

| RACE | Evergreen | Magistri | Pachena |
|---|---|---|---|
| *3rd Inshore* | | | |
| Date: Tues., Aug. 7 | 53rd | 39th | 48th |
| Distance: 32 miles | | | |
| Winds: SW 13–25 knots, | | | |
| Rain squalls | | | |
| *Fastnet[2]* | | | |
| Date: Sat., Aug. 11 | DNF | 20th | DNF |
| Distance: 605 miles | | | |
| Winds: Light–60 knots, | | | |
| gusting 70 knots | | | |
| Overall Standing out of | 54th | 33rd | 51st |
| 57 boats | | | |

[1] Double points
[2] Triple points

# Sources

## Books

Apter, Michael. *The Dangerous Edge: The Psychology of Excitement*. New York: The Free Press, 1992.

Bennett, Glin. *Beyond Endurance: Survival at the Extremes*. London: Secker and Warburg, 1983.

Coffey, Maria. *Where the Mountain Casts Its Shadow: The Dark Side of Extreme Adventure*. New York: St. Martin's Press, 2003.

Coles, Adlard. *Heavy Weather Sailing*, Third Revised Edition. Clinton Corners, N.Y.: John De Graff, 1981.

Dugard, Martin. *Knockdown: The Harrowing Account of a Yacht Race Turned Deadly*. New York: Pocket Books, 1999.

Gonzales, Laurence. *Deep Survival: Who Lives, Who Dies and Why*. New York: W.W. Norton & Co., 2005.

Henderson, Richard. *Singlehanded Sailing: The Experiences and Techniques of the Lone Voyagers*. 2nd Edition. Camden, Maine: International Marine, 1992.

Hunter, Doug. *Against the Odds: The Incredible Story of Evergreen and the Canada's Cup*. Toronto: Personal Library, 1981.

Lundy, Derek. *Godforsaken Sea: Racing the World's Most Dangerous Waters*. Toronto: Seal Books, 1998.

Moitessier, Bernard. *The Long Way*. New York: Sheridan House, 2000.

Rousmaniere, John. *Fastnet, Force 10: The Deadliest Storm in the History of Modern Sailing*. New York: W.W. Norton, 2000.

Van Dorn, William. *Oceanography and Seamanship*. New York: Dodd, Mead and Co., 1974.

## Magazines

Butler, David, et al. "A Race Against Death." *Newsweek*, August 27, 1979.

Farlinger, Peter. "From Aboard Magistri." *Sailing Canada*, Nov./Dec. 1979.

Fitzpatrick, John. "From Aboard Evergreen." *Sailing Canada*, Nov./Dec. 1979.

Jarman, Colin. "Admiral's Cup: The Report." *Sailing Canada*, Nov./Dec. 1979.

Knights, Jack. "Aussies claim Admiral's Cup." *Canadian Yachting*, October 1979.

Newton, John. "Surviving the Fastnet Blow." *Pacific Yachting*, November 1979.

"An Awesome Warning from the Sea." *Sports Illustrated*, August 27, 1979.

"Death in the South Irish Sea." *Time Magazine*, August 27, 1979.

"Fastnet Disaster." *Pacific Yachting*. October 1979.

"The Storm Force Fastnet." *Sail*. October 1979.